Death's Gift

*

Chapters on Resurrection
and Bereavement

*

NICHOLAS PETER HARVEY

EPWORTH PRESS

© Epworth Press 1985

British Library Cataloguing-in-Publication Data available

7162 0411 8

First published 1985
by Epworth Press
Room 195, 1 Central Buildings
Westminster, London SW1

Typeset at The Spartan Press Ltd, Lymington, Hants
Printed in Great Britain by
Richard Clay (The Chaucer Press) Ltd,
Bungay, Suffolk

For my parents

Contents

Acknowledgments and a Cautionary Note   vii

Part One

1   Bearings   3
2   The Wounded Self   13

Part Two

3   The Chosen   23
4   Permission to Flee   29
5   Peter   35
6   The Beloved Disciple Remembers   39
7   Orphaning, Judgment and Glorification   48
8   Seeing Again   56
9   Joy   65

Part Three

10   Neither Martyr nor Suicide   75
11   The Poor, Sinners and the Sinless Man   83
12   Death-spasm   90
13   The Hinge of Memory   98
14   The Future of Memory   107
15   Dead Ends   111

Part Four

16   What Difference Does It Make?   121
17   Predisposition and Revelation   130
18   Real Presence   137

Notes   145

Acknowledgments and a Cautionary Note

Without the generosity of the Queen's College, Birmingham, in granting me a Research Fellowship in 1978 and in renewing it until 1980, work on this book would not have been sustained in a setting which proved ideal. So many people at Queen's have given me warm encouragement and stimulus that it is almost invidious to select names.

Yet there are particular debts which I want to acknowledge. Two Principals of widely differing styles gave me unstinted and unofficious support: Anthony Bird and Gordon S. Wakefield. Geoffrey Wainwright brought an acute mind and a distillation of vast reading to bear in saving me from ineptitudes and pointing out directions the work might take. John Munsey Turner was generous with editorial suggestions and wholeheartedly kept me at it at seemingly unproductive moments. Particular kinds of moral support came from Malcolm Prescott and other members of the tutorial staff, past and present. Several students gave very special help, notably David Wynford Thomas, Stephen Toze, John Prysor-Jones, Richard Worsley and Derek Cottrill. A succession of Queen's wives typed various drafts: Mary Brown, Jane Hall, Alison Toze, Sheila Howard, Caroline Raynor and Carole Smith. All were most kind, conscientious and efficient.

The book had its genesis before I came to Queen's. Seminal contributions to the underlying thinking came from Luke Suart, Sebastian Moore, Kevin Maguire, Dominic Barthelémy and James Suart, with whom I conversed at such length that I am not sure whether the foundational hunch mentioned in the first chapter is his or mine. Latterly John Stokes laboured long and hard in sharpening up many of the chapters, and David Ford had a clarifying influence. To Miss Violet Elliott of Stoke by Clare I owe access to the little-known poetry of W. R. Rogers, and the boost which her affection and humour always give. I discovered Arthur Mielke's book through the good offices of Paul Rowntree Clifford.

The brief dedication hints at a debt beyond words to my parents. Inexpressible acknowledgment is likewise owed to the monks of Downside Abbey, past and present; and to James Suart, his first wife Priscilla and their six children. An inestimable contribution of a quite different but connected kind was made, almost entirely without their knowing it, by the ecumenical prayer group at St Mark's, Hamilton Gardens, NW8 and the one founded by Gae Twomey in Edgbaston; and by Harry and Raffé Stobart and Christopher Neil-Smith.

This is not in the strict sense a scholarly book, its thrust being best described as obliquely pastoral; but I have endeavoured to acknowledge written sources in the text and notes. Biblical quotations are sometimes from the RSV, sometimes from the Jerusalem Bible, occasionally from the King James Version, and sometimes from the Douai version on which I was reared. I should not wish to be aligned unreservedly with any particular school in the field of biblical studies or with any 'party line' in systematic theology. A product of the only ecumenical college in the land, I would hope the book is ecumenical in this as in other senses. The conclusions are entirely my own, and I must ask the reader's indulgence towards any blind spots and insensitivities which may have survived even the rigorous scrutiny of my two Methodist tutors and other advisers already mentioned.

The Queen's College   *Nicholas Peter Harvey*
Edgbaston
Birmingham

Part One

I

Bearings

Bereavement is fashionable, but resurrection is not. The increased attention paid in recent years to problems linked with bereavement has not been matched by any comparable focussing on the theme of resurrection. This incongruity puts a very pointed question to the Christian churches as to the power of their witness to resurrection. It would be churlish to decry the sensitive and sophisticated work done in analysing the states of mind of bereaved people in the light of modern psychology.[1] But if the shape of death is to be considered at an appropriate depth there is a pressing need to set these findings in the perspective provided by the resurrection of Jesus. There is an equally urgent need to look at resurrection anew in the light of data about bereavement. This book was born out of puzzled and painful awareness of a neglected area here, just where the good news of Jesus Christ theoretically finds its very heart and centre.

There are, as I discovered when once embarked on this quest, other elements of incongruity. It is arguable that even the majority of professing Christians have at best a purely notional belief in an after-life;[2] while the fashionable style of biblical scholarship is frankly sceptical about the story of the empty tomb and embarrassed by the resurrection narratives as they stand.[3] The irony is that this scepticism and embarrassment are largely in the name of modern knowledge, while characteristically modern accounts of bereavement, whether analytical or personal, are scarcely noticed when resurrection is being considered.

'Never the twain shall meet': pastoral concern with bereavement continues to be dominated by the social welfare mentality, thus failing, unlike Agatha in T. S. Eliot's *The Family Reunion*,[4] 'to discover some meaning in death'. Meanwhile those who write of the resurrection of Jesus with reference to the New Testament narratives read largely like those addressed by Harry in the same play as

> . . . people
> to whom nothing has happened . . .

Ostensibly interpreting the texts, most work of this kind reduces Jesus and the disciples to ciphers, so that the story is devitalized at the very point where, if we stay with the Gospel writers, it is most vibrantly alive. I state the matter thus strongly not by way of a cheap jibe but because all too often such writing is taken as authoritative, as the best the church has to say these days about resurrection. It is my hope that the following pages will at least hint at how much more there is to be said.

On the other hand, much traditional catechesis has implied that raising a man from the dead would have been no problem for God, however or wherever or whenever. This blanket emphasis on God's almighty power, with Jesus' resurrection as merely the biggest and best miracle of the lot, undermines the theme of relationship and is therefore alienating. We need to seek the appropriateness of this event of resurrection happening to that particular person at that time in that particular human setting, with special regard to the disciples' states of heart and mind.

What kind of power is this which, it is claimed, expressed itself supremely in God's self-emptying for man's sake in the passion and death of Jesus? God, who 'has first loved us', went all the way in order to convince mankind of his unfaltering love. What kind of experience lay behind this claim? What abiding reality for the disciples had this ultimate self-emptying of God? If these considerations are to acquire any salvific purchase on our hearts and minds, far more is at stake than merely a moment when it may have seemed to a group of benighted people that their God had vanished into the void. In the New

Testament the idea that in becoming man the Son emptied himself is unqualified. Likewise the idea that the Father gave up the Son, surrendering him to human life *and death*. Clearly these convictions emerge from contact with Jesus. St John tells us that Jesus, 'having loved his own, loved them to the end.' Not 'a seeming end', but 'the end'.

It might be objected that as the entire New Testament was written after the resurrection, this finality should not be over-interpreted. The full dimensions of the cataclysm were only realized when the joy of the resurrection took up residence in the hearts of the chosen ones. We do not have a neat stage-by-stage record of their successive states of mind. The evangelists and the other canonical writers have theologized the passion. This objection can be sustained, provided that the conclusion is not drawn that my enquiry is rendered abortive by lack of biblical evidence. A theologized narrative is one which is enriched by revelatory hindsight; there is no good reason to think that such enrichment militates against historical accuracy. A deeper and more comprehensive insight into what was happening in no way threatens precise memory of past events, particularly of a critical and even traumatic nature. This is a point which will receive more leisured attention in some subsequent chapters, as it is fundamental to my whole attitude to the matter in hand. Its mention at this early stage is in order to put down a marker in a very controversial area.

Perspective is lost if we make of Jesus' death something so completely incommensurate with any other loss as to deprive it of all intelligibility. This is not to deny the fittingness of the tradition which puts into Jesus' mouth the rhetorical question, 'Is there any sorrow like unto my sorrow?' Yet if we start from there as an unexamined assumption, we give ourselves no chance to pick up the deepest resonance of these words, particularly in their consequences for the disciples. This work began with a hunch that comparisons can be made between what happens in bereavement and what happened to the disciples; it has developed through a growing awareness that the New Testament record enables such comparisons to be drawn much more richly and revealingly than my hunch allowed for. Later chapters fill out my conviction that only in the stretching of our hearts and minds by the deployment of the widest available range of such comparisons will the distinctive nature of what happened to the disciples declare itself to us. We can then, and only then, 'place' all other deaths and bereavements in organic relation to the disciples' passage from the suffering of an unprecedented desolation into the peace of God.

The verb 'place' appears here in inverted commas because what is really happening as this picture shapes up in us is a realization of true connections, of what is the case. The role of faith and prayer in this realization is of course indispensable: such an integrated perception cannot be simply read off from the 'bare facts' of the Gospel story considered in relation to whatever we can glean of other bereavements. 'No man by taking thought can add to his stature a single cubit.' That having been said, it must be added that pursuit of the exploration outlined in this book has played its part in convincing me more than notionally of the resurrection of Jesus,[5] and therefore of the universal repercussions of his death on the cross. Through this quest has come a strong sense of the radical link between all life, death and bereavement on the one hand and the story of the disciples on the other.

To do justice both to the links and to the differentiating factors between the disciples' bereavement and all others we need to hold in view as fully as possible both the New Testament record of the bereaved disciples' witness and a range of other bereavement testimonies.[6] We need to give both types of witness ample breathing-space in ourselves to facilitate their creative interplay in our hearts and minds. Otherwise our pastoral models of bereavement are liable to be narrowly humanistic, while the first believers' experience of the death and resurrection of Jesus will remain in a sealed compartment remote from life and impervious to the heart's search for enlargement and the mind's probe towards comprehensive intelligibility.

There is a danger of developing an increasingly sophisticated psychological and sociological analysis of bereavement in terms which offer some degree of descriptive clarity but no healing, while the religious dimension enters only by way of pietistic intimations which do not effectively penetrate the particular anguish and joy of being bereaved. How many people, one wonders, have been bruised or repelled by being glibly told that all is well because the Lord is risen, without any suggestion of either the heights or the depths through which the disciples went in being brought to the point where they could joyfully make that salvific proclamation. Words of would-be reassurance without any proper context are prone to induce or heighten guilt and despair in the bereaved, for whom the bald proclamation as commonly stated does not hint a connection with or a healing commentary on a bewildered loss of moorings. Bereavement can be a launching into an irreversible joy; but it can also become no more than learning survival techniques. These enable 'normal' life to proceed at the price of postponing the quest for meaning and leaving the 'survivor' radically a problem to himself and others, whatever the surface appearance of coping.

The church proclaims the life of Jesus as the decisive life, and his death as constituting a radically new relationship between God and all creation. This interpretation of Jesus developed in his followers after his death, in their bereavement, which is therefore the seed-bed of the church. It is a commonplace to say that the Gospels were written from a resurrection perspective. It needs also to be said that a peculiarly devastating experience of bereavement accompanied the birth of the disciples' belief in Jesus' resurrection. There was no return to the innocent security of the time before Calvary, when they relied passively on the Lord's visible presence. When stressing the fact that the disciples were bereaved, I once received the puzzled reply: 'But it was for a very short time!' This idea that their bereavement lasted only three days seems to me to falsify the New Testament evidence.

There is no undoing the death of Jesus, which the resurrection itself declares to be the saving event. Far from cancelling his death, the resurrection proclaims its full significance. In showing forth the meaning of Jesus' life and death, the resurrection does not remove the scandal and folly of the cross.

It is precisely this stumbling-block, this foolishness, which is pin-pointed and writ large by the resurrection. Otherwise the risen Christ is merely another idol rather than the saving victim.

It is not just anybody whom the New Testament proclaims as risen: it is the disgraced and crucified Jesus, a man condemned and executed. The resurrection declares that there, in the dreadful end-game played by the Jewish authorities, Pilate and the people, is the place of revelation, the ultimate act of love, the beginning of the transformation of all created being into praise and glory. That death, that sacrifice, that obedient self-giving in unknowing and powerless love, is shown to be not merely acceptable but redemptive, healing and making whole, binding up man's self-inflicted wounds and empowering each of us in the way of love to become a person for ever.[7]

If, then, the death of Jesus was the decisive death, the bereavement of the disciples was the decisive bereavement. If 'God was in Christ, reconciling the world to himself', the bereavement of Christ's followers was in essence the world's bereavement. Peter followed after those who arrested Jesus 'to see the end'. There is a terrible finality, emptiness and loss in these words. When Jesus died Pilate and Herod, rulers of the old world, became friends in a complicity of the damned.[8]

It is my intention to explore the resurrection-meaning of Christ's death as joyously proclaimed by his bereaved friends and followers to be the decisive event in mankind's history and indeed in the life of the cosmos, the power and wisdom of God making all things new. His death as the victory over all that holds us back from our true self-hood and vocation as 'sons of God and joint heirs with Christ'. His death as effectively expressing an all-encompassing love quite beyond explanation or rationalization, ensuring that all things co-operate unto good, that our sins are forgiven and our evil cast out without limit or condition.

I shall also consider the dying and death of a Christian as being a channel of the risen life of Christ for those involved: a further specification and nurturing of that life which is in us by baptism but needs to be realized progressively throughout life as we are freed from slavery to the things of this world to serve the living God. There is a degree of identification or parallelism, if you will, between the death of Jesus and the death of a faithful believer. There are bereavement experiences which witness to this identification, freshly affirming the Godwardness of this or that person while freeing the bereaved from the danger of imprisonment in a moment of the past.

Both the similarities and the differences between such experiences and the disciples' bereavement will be indicated. In stressing the uniquely decisive character of the latter, I should wish to present other bereavements as furthering our awareness of the very total and totally personal implications of Christ's death. Some people say that bereavement has made clear to them for the first time what the New Testament means by resurrection; others, that the New Testament has enabled them to cope with their bereavement. There is no reason to suppose a contradiction here. The issue is the life-giving, releasing, affirmatory quality of dying, of death and of bereavement in the spirit of Christ. Each person being unique, each death and each bereavement accepted in his spirit[9] becomes a contribution to the building-up of the body of Christ. This acceptance has nothing to do with mere resignation, everything to do with the creative power of God 'bringing into being the things that are not', both in the dying and in the bereaved.

Just as in the disciples' lives the end turned out to be the beginning, so is it with other bereavements. No loss can be more total than theirs. There is a rupture, a discontinuity, a disintegration. Our belief is in a raising from the dead, not in a serene survival or evasion of death. The Gospel accounts record the extremely disorientating effects on the disciples of Jesus' passion, death and resurrection. At every stage they are presented as labouring with a whole spectrum of emotions. The resurrection was not a backward-looking consolation but a strengthening of faith and a summons to mission: it drew the disciples out of this-worldly security into a new and very risky way of life.

The objection might be raised that very few people have the kind of bereavement dealt with here. Yet even if it could be proved conclusively that there is nothing creative, at least at the conscious level, in the bereavement experience of the vast majority of mankind, nothing would be changed. Our concern is with what Christ's death *is*, not what people think or fail to think about it. If his death is the world's bereavement and the world's transformation, begun in him and yet awaited, there is an important sense in which it does not matter how many people are yet aware of this power at work, of this current of risen life.

Christ's death is for all, but it is not our conscious advertence to that fact that makes it so. Those to whom this truth is revealed are the spearhead of the true world-change: they are mankind's consciousness of the working-out of that redemption which is potentially all men's possession. This redemption is a theological fact unrelated to statistics. Our normal condition is to be redeemed, to be living the death of Christ until he comes. The comparative rarity of the condition, at least according to human judgment, in no way invalidates its normative status, unless we yield our judgment to the spirit of this world, which is eminently statistical. It is what God is making of man that matters, not what man makes of himself.

Christ's death seen in the light of his resurrection re-interprets all human dying, reversing this world's perspective at the point of maximum negativity. Having witnessed the enactment of the world's sin at Jesus' expense, an enactment resulting in the world's bereavement, the disciples are brought into the consciousness of the risen Lord in two senses. While they are made aware of him as raised from the dead, they begin to be conformed to his risen mind. Their contact with the risen Christ, confirmed by the Holy Spirit, empowered them for the work of man's salvation – a task which we inherit and which presses urgently upon us in the face of so much evil. If we have even glimpsed the atonement, the love-powered one-ing of worlds, how are we straitened until our part is accomplished.

The bereavement experiences to be considered have in common awareness of the dead person as more fully alive, more truly and richly himself or herself than ever before. Such awareness is at an opposite pole from the type of communication which occurs at a séance,[10] which holds the bereaved in a frozen posture towards the dead rather than encouraging them to enter on the next stage of their own life's journey freed from the constraints of the past.

Those people, dying or dead, who are perceived by us, however intermittently, as 'in the Spirit' become for us radiations of God's love, of his grace, of his life for us and in us. Such people are rays of light converging on a single source, the unity and purpose of all things. This influence properly understood draws us towards that source, draws us into the life of the Holy Trinity. They are at one with the source, but are not themselves the source.

If this distinction becomes blurred idolatry supervenes, and Christ is divided. This blurring results in a double confusion: in addition to identifying the saints with God, we are blinded to their personal inadequacies. Only one human person, Jesus, was fully in the Spirit. He is the norm, and no other. Other people's light can irradiate him for us, but it can never substitute for him without paralysis. The communion of saints is nothing if not the work of Christ.

It is appropriate that this cautionary note should occur here, for what goes wrong, not being central to my theme, will not loom large in later chapters. Things can and do go wrong; but interpretation in the Spirit both of the deaths of those close to us and of the New Testament converges in the realization that since the crucifixion death is no longer a disaster, but can be known as a step into fuller life for both the deceased and the bereaved.

The connections outlined in these chapters came to me as a gift rather than as a direct result of a standard reasoning process. While thought is of course involved, the patterns emerged as a distillation by the Holy Spirit out of things happening in my own and others' lives. Such a gift needs and seeks to be more widely shared – why otherwise is it given? These reflections are therefore offered in the hope that they may be of some help to some people. For me the whole topic came alive when I began to correlate and contrast the disciples' witness to what happened to them with the witness of bereaved people. What was the death of Jesus in the disciples' experience? What is it to be bereaved? In this form these are modern questions, requiring answers which must do justice to both areas of inquiry. These are the two polarities of all that follows.

2

The Wounded Self

In speaking of bereavement people often talk of 'getting over it', 'accepting it', or even 'living with it'; although it is rarely the bereaved who use such phrases, at least with conviction. To what does this language refer? The death itself? The sorrow and sense of loss felt over the death? The difficulties of carrying on normal life afterwards? Uncertainty about the fate of the departed one? Probably all of these aspects are implied, but such phrases suggest that whatever the 'it' is, it is static: you do the getting over, while that over which you get remains fixed, like a hurdle in a race. Some bereaved people lend a degree of credibility to this image by compulsively talking about the dead as if they were still exactly what they were. Such people are accordingly judged not to have got over it, but even in such cases, or at such moments, the witness to bereavement has a great deal more to offer.

It is questionable whether understanding is furthered rather than hindered by looking at bereavement as a problem, as has been the tendency in most books on the subject in the last fifteen years. Much fascinating material has been amassed, systematized and made available to a wider public. It is a curious and revealing fact that the great value of this work is commonly vitiated by the notion that the problem is the loss of the loved one, with the consequence that this loss, with all its pyschological concomitants, is seen as a huge obstacle to be crossed only with the utmost difficulty. The future tends to be conceived largely in terms of discovering survival techniques in a world which for the bereaved is drastically diminished. The enriching and even transforming effects of bereavement are not denied, but they are remarkably under-emphasized. There is a sense of a pre-ordained process of adjustment to which each bereavement conforms more or less successfully. The dominant emphasis on a particular psychological model of the stages within this process, coupled with attention to the various caring agencies available, subtly contradicts the mysterious opportunity which bereavement presents.[1]

To consider bereavement in such a way suggests that it is the death of a loved person which makes the bereaved problematical to himself and to his world. In refreshing contrast is the view of a bereaved friend whom I shall call Richard:

> What is the wound of bereavement? Is there an inevitable wound which is bereavement, which is an inescapable occurrence of that condition? I begin to doubt . . . 'The wound of bereavement' is in fact myself, that part of me which is my cross, which is always with me even though I may learn to live with it, etc. Bereavement doesn't bring it about as a new factor in my life. However, the death of someone brings the significance of my own life into relief, and highlights my cross, highlights the limitations of me, and as a part of finding the direction of my future life that which is myself in all its rawness comes to the forefront of my mind. The loss of the other person in fact reveals to what a large extent one hid behind them, leant upon them, relied upon them, used them . . . It doesn't help to hide behind the myth that what in fact is myself I am calling bereavement.[2]

This is a starting point dramatically different from, although not in absolute contradiction to, what it is now becoming fashionable to call 'the grief process'.[3] The background for this more positive analysis is a clear awareness of an abiding presence of the deceased, a transformed and transforming presence of a quality unmistakably other than what this person was seen to be before death. Other than, but not less than. More real because made whole, integrated, no longer bound by those limitations which used to loom so large and for which this person was often adversely judged. This is a wholly and truly loving presence, offering no nostalgic comfort but a developing

release from the constraints of clinging and therefore ambivalent dependence in the past.

The truth and fullness of the relationship is no longer in
doubt. The nagging insecurities focussed on the beloved before
death no longer have any place, any reality. Thus the future,
however imponderable, can be envisaged with equanimity in
the strength which the newly abiding presence mediates. The
relationship remains central, but now is focussed on and
beginning to release the potential of the 'survivor' for future
growth. In these terms, to return to the image with which this
chapter began, there is no hurdle to be got over: there is only a
new freedom in relationship, indivisibly with the deceased and
with others.

This is not meant to imply that no difficulties exist or arise,
nor that everything in the garden is already lovely. My
contention is that the death of a loved person is at root a
growing-point, with all the pain and struggle which that phrase
suggests. It is undeniable, and indeed central to this picture of
death, that there is a self-exposure promoted by the tearing
away of a prop. The distinction at stake is not between a
painless separation and a painful one, but between bereavement seen as a genuinely critical, creative moment or phase in a
person's development, and bereavement relegated to the less-
than-human category of things to be got over. This latter way of
picturing the matter suggests a salvage operation, a stoical
return to 'normality', rather than a boundless opportunity, an
opening up to God, to one's true self, to all that was and is and is
to be.

'Death is the great revealer . . . when death comes we realize,
as we never thought we would, that it is a terrible thing to fall
into the hands of the living God.' These words, unlike those of
most of my witnesses, were written by a man who had no
advance warning of his wife's death. Far from contradicting my
thesis, his words strengthen it by corroborating a particular
emphasis. Caught by surprise by his sudden bereavement,
Arthur Mielke thereafter experienced grief in all its complexity,
including 'resentment, anger, frustration, guilt, fear, bewilderment, and an aching loneliness'. He quotes with approval the

view that 'separation anxiety' is at the very centre of grief.[4]

The question 'separation from what?' needs to be asked. Separation from the person who has died, or separation from our version of that person? Is it the loss of the reality of the other person which torments the bereaved, or is it the loss of the other as embodying my security in this world? If it is the removal of an anchor in this latter sense which causes the pain, the traumatic element in bereavement can then be characterized as symptomatic of withdrawal from idolatry. Whatever elements of inappropriate dependence were present in the relationship now declare themselves more clearly and agonizingly than before as needing to be cast out. This is not to claim that any relationship which includes such elements is a bad thing. All human relationships are mixed blessings until the Second Coming, when they will take on their proper proportions in our lives. The clinging, idolatrous tendency remains until the end: it, rather than bereavement as such, is the problem. The bereavement is the occasion rather than the cause of the difficulty.

In thus provoking withdrawal symptoms, bereavement offers an opportunity for growth. An opportunity, not a guaranteed process: Queen Victoria's life-long static devotion to her husband's memory dramatically illustrates that the potential of bereavement can be arrested. The bereaved person may remain locked in a stage of the relationship which was perhaps appropriate in the past but is now a sign of imprisonment. Such a person seeks to perpetuate the relationship as it was, ironically in the name of fidelity to the departed one. While the conventional wisdom continues to speak in non-explanatory terms of 'getting over' or 'not getting over' a bereavement, it is more accurate to speak of allowing yourself to die to one form of presence and one mode of relationship in order that a deeper reality can be expressed and confirmed. The same point is made more incisively if it is said that the bereaved needs to let the deceased die.

Much that goes wrong in bereavement stems from an inability or refusal to do this. Letting the beloved die involves letting go of that in oneself which seeks to continue to cling to the beloved as a focus of false security. There is, then, a need to surrender an inadequate version of the person who has died; but that need in its turn requires the surrender of aspects of oneself hitherto regarded as constitutive of one's being. The distresses involved in being freed from this type of security-seeking are growing pains. To fall into the hands of the living God may well be terrible in the sense of that word no longer current, but it can hardly be bad, as Mielke would be the first to admit.

'And Jacob awaked out of his sleep, and he said, "Surely the Lord is in this place, and I knew it not." And he was afraid, and said, "How *dreadful* is this place! this is none other but the house of God, and this is the gate of heaven"' (Gen. 28. 16–17). The 1611 version has been deliberately chosen for this quotation: the word 'dreadful', which I have underlined, gives a stronger and more apt sense, if taken as 'full of dread', than the alternatives of more modern translators, 'awesome', 'fearsome' and 'awe-inspiring'. Jacob's experience is at one and the same time of dread and of privilege: indeed it is of one as the sign of the other. The place which is full of dread, the place where he feels out of his depth, is recognized as the gate of heaven. Likewise the bereaved can come to recognize the anxiety and fear characteristic of bereavement as significant not so much in terms of loss as of opportunity, with new space for the living Lord, an opportunity which has about it still a degree of ambivalence. Thus the disciples who met the risen Jesus at the lakeside were afraid to ask who he was *because they knew*. The inertial tendency so pervasive in creation must resist any rumour of angels,[5] and still more of resurrection.

The opportunity offered by bereavement is decisive enough, but in this world's terms contradictory, for it is a call on to a new and very exposed path with alarmingly few signposts and familiar reassurances. It is hardly to be wondered at that there is some baulking at such an open prospect, that the gate of heaven is not always felt to be compellingly attractive, that it can seem safer to cling in heart, mind and imagination to that familiar form of relationship which in the nature of things has already come to an end in death. There can be no rule of thumb for the avoidance of this fixation and for the following of the new way of dangerous freedom which beckons the bereaved.

Remember the incident of the rich and virtuous young man who was advised by Jesus to give up all he owned. This young man went away sorrowful, 'for he had many possessions'. 'Where your treasure house is, there will your heart be also.' For all his virtue this man found himself unable, at that time at least, to give up his dependence on material security, and so could not find it in his heart to take the opportunity of following Jesus. There is no condemnation, only the sadness of a chance not taken. Similarly with the bereaved: there is no forcing, only the chance to opt for a new way the contours of which can then begin to reveal themselves. In one way or another the issue is always a fuller, more authentic life. 'To be or not to be.' It is impossible to chose not to be; but to remain in the shoals is a tragic plight for as long as it lasts, not least because it is very habit-forming.

In preparing the disciples for his death Jesus stresses their existing faith and the need for prayerful vigilance to avoid being pulled off course. The possibility of regressive or escapist behaviour is real enough in bereavement, as at all crisis-points, so that it is vital to keep the focus on what is really happening. Faith, vigilance and prayer alone can ensure that the memory of the dead person is not denied, cheapened, romanticized or fossilized – in other words that the survivor's interpretative faculties are kept supple and his receptive capacity enlarged. Otherwise there is no adequate disposition for resurrection, not because you have not earned such a revelation (nobody has!) but because you are unable to perceive it.

It is not my purpose to elucidate, even if I could, *how* a bereaved person can move through enriching heights and purgative depths into a much deeper communication than ever before with all that is. It is rather a matter of drawing attention to the fact that such developments occur; and that testimonies to this effect suggest a shape or thrust in bereavement quite contrary to the 'normal' picture of picking up as best you may your life's shattered pieces. We are concerned with a sense of the dead person as so newly and purely alive that the bereaved one can never be the same again.

Thus Mielke, noting that his wife is now more real, and a more real influence upon him, than before her death, proceeds to comment: 'I could never have believed that this would be true, but it is . . . Never before did I really understand how a person who has died physically could be so alive, so powerfully alive. I am beginning to understand the amazing influence of the risen Christ on Paul, for I am just learning what it really means to be caught up in the liberating sway of one who has crossed over the line from death to life, as Paul put it.'[6] These words are especially pointed in that they are written by a man whose journal unguardedly reveals the depths of his dereliction in the months after his wife's death. In stressing the positive outcome Mielke neither distances nor diminishes the desolating sense of loss so often interwoven with bereavement, especially in the early stages. None of my witnesses is proposing *alternatives* to grief. All have suffered too deeply for facile optimism to have any place. All would certainly agree with Neville Ward: '"Getting over" calamity is not at all a good idea. It is to empty intense and formidable experience of meaning and reduce it to the status of an interruption.'[7]

Part Two

3

The Chosen

It is significant that Jesus wrote nothing and saw no need to leave written records. His revelation was initially manifested to his chosen ones, and in its fullness only to his closest companions, whose witness is the catalyst of our faith. St Paul and others who were not of this company soon developed the implications of this witness in the light of their own links with the risen Christ. But the foundation of the church is the testimony of the bereaved disciples. If Christ as the manifestation of God is to be properly placed in his human setting it must be stressed that the authoritative witness to him comes from a group of bereaved people, comes indeed out of their bereavement. Although Jesus ate and drank with them after he was raised from the dead, the form of their previous earthly companionship with him was never resumed. The New Testament resurrection narratives make clear that he has entered upon a new way of being which is as yet uniquely his. He is with them in a new way and therefore in the old terms remote from them. They are and remain bereaved.

Modern exegesis has done a great service by drawing attention to a most remarkable change in the disciples. What happened at Easter is not merely something out there but something in them. These twin happenings, to Jesus and to them, are indivisible in terms of their relationship with him or, better, his with them. Having lost him in his death they are found by him in his rising, and to him they respond. But that to which they testify is Jesus raised from the dead, not a mere feat of 'consciousness-raising' performed by God upon themselves and enabling them to be suddenly optimistic about the outcome of the cross. The New Testament gives no support to the view that faith created the appearances of the risen Lord, who had to work very hard indeed to convince them, to reassure them and to energize them for their future missionary task.

The fact that Jesus does not at this stage appear to complete outsiders hardly supports the idea that his followers' wishful thinking projected itself in the form of apparitions. To any but his bereaved disciples such appearances would have been merely arbitrary or undesirable phenomena. Only those who had been brought by Jesus before his crucifixion to a point of no return could be expected to receive and respond to his risen presence. The risen Jesus could presumably have appeared to anybody; but to imply a deficiency in the resurrection in that he did not do so is an unwarranted removal of the Lord from his historical context and a trivializing of his relationships.

The witnesses are already chosen before the crucifixion, set apart for a special task of mission not yet made clear to them. His relationship with his chosen ones is crucial in the beginnings of the church, not primarily for their sakes but for the sake of the spreading of the good news. Only those who had been his closest companions were ready, even perhaps despite themselves, for this task of inaugurating the body of Christ in the world. To suggest otherwise means that it does not really matter who was raised from the dead, while the New Testament's whole point is that the risen one was the crucified Jesus.

It is possible to fall victim to the notion that the disciples had a built-in and almost unfair advantage. This is to treat the resurrection appearances, and the gift of the Spirit, as sweets for the children. They were in fact thus 'privileged', if this term is at all appropriate, in the light of the special and very onerous responsibilities they were to exercise, and in continuity with all their previous communication with Jesus. The difficulty dissolves when it is realized that the root of the church is the relationship between Jesus and this group, a relationship of very considerable intensity which had developed through diverse and not infrequently explosive experiences to a point of searing finality in his killing and their flight.

It is precisely because of the hope of the kingdom he had

aroused and confirmed in them that his death has for them a comprehensive finality which it could not have at the time for anyone else. His death was the end of their world, the end of their expectation. It was sheer and irreparable loss, leaving them in a limbo with no way out in any direction. They thus consciously experienced what was in fact the case for all humanity. Their master, the sinless one, had engaged man's desperation at its very heart, and had met only dereliction. He had taken his stand 'in total, final solidarity between man and God; turning to God, he is man and stands condemned; turning to man he is God and stands rejected'.[1] Thus he had to die, and his followers, having come so far with him, were immersed in that dereliction. 'This is your hour, and the power of darkness,' said Jesus to his captors. This was a cosmic darkness, into which his followers were consciously plunged. Their bad record of misunderstanding, slowness of heart and attempted short-cuts to the establishment of the kingdom had already burgeoned into craven flight from the eye of the storm where he had been and they now found only themselves, having thus far, and ironically, failed to perceive that the eye of the storm is always the place of peace.[2]

There is no suggestion in the New Testament that they had any special strength, any possibility of coping with this bereavement. They were themselves alone, hapless, confused, fearful. Nothing that is said about the resurrection should be allowed to take the edge off their plight, uprooted as they were from all earlier securities. This is not to belittle the fact, made clear by John's Gospel in particular, that Jesus prepared them for his death. It is to say that they could not face this reality, so that this preparation bore fruit only in response to his resurrection. 'My strength finds its full scope in your weakness.'

The resurrection does not deny the rupture which was the cross, this nothingness of evil triumphant, good men deprived of hope, a world buried in impenetrable night. If no other human life is comparable to that of Jesus, no other human desolation is comparable to his friends' loss of him. Unlike all earlier prophets Jesus had firmly identified the kingdom with himself. What happened at Easter was a new creation, a creative act of God who raised Jesus from the dead, bringing new life out of nothing. '. . . our search for the conditions under which there arose the proclamation of Jesus' resurrection draws a blank *on all decisive points*' (my italics).[3]

Indications of resurrection belief or hope in the Old Testament and inter-testamentary period offer something very shadowy and remote, in no way able to match the startling immediacy, originality, intensity and scope of the picture of the kingdom already embodied in Jesus' ministry. People touched, however confusedly, by this extraordinary newness of life, could hardly have drawn strength of purpose in their loss from those thin and twilight intimations. Jesus had already taken them beyond that kind of hope, which would have been merely a regression, a turning back from the whole drive of their life with him. There was no framework of images to enable his followers to anticipate or create the resurrection. Until the risen Lord impinged overwhelmingly upon them their game was up, their future blank, their recent past an irreversible but delusive enchantment. Titus Groan fought 'anchored darkness',[4] but the disciples were oppressed by a deeper gloom, the horrific ending in blood of a kingdom which had scarcely begun.

This is not to deny that in the light of the resurrection past, present and future acquired for them a clear shape. This is very much the point: it was the resurrection itself which gave the shape,[5] the meaning, the purpose, which reinterpreted the dereliction. In proclaiming the risen Lord the apostles proclaim the crucifixion as the place of mankind's forgiveness, the beginning of a completely new way of being man, 'God's way to be man', as the title of a recent book has it.[6] In so speaking they know themselves reborn as the vanguard of a forgiven humanity on the way to resurrection. Deprived of his earthly companionship they now know a deeper fellowship with Jesus in the power of the Holy Spirit. The risen Lord who is with the Father is by virtue of that fact more real to them than in his earthly life. Their relationship with him is no longer one of clinging and bemused dependence but of trustful sharing. Through his death declared in power by his resurrection they begin to have his mind, to share his strength in being conformed to him.

They remember and see now as appropriate his words 'It is expedient for you that I go.' Their Lord lives for them and in them with unprecedented richness and depth of meaning on the other side of the chasm of meaninglessness which his death had seemed to be. Mark's Gospel records starkly, almost brutally, the failure of the disciples at every point of Jesus' ministry. Their bereavement brings this impotence to a head and takes them beyond it into the freedom of the sons of God which is the risen Lord's gift to them. The bereavement is not reversed but shown as the way forward for them, an initiation into the meaning and power of Jesus as Saviour. It is in and through their bereavement that Jesus is shown to them as not merely *their* Lord and master, *their* prophet and messiah, but the effective Lord of all creation whose work of atonement, consummated on the cross, will through their agency bring all men to the Father.

Their loss, then, does not create the risen Lord, but is the indispensable setting for his true scale and substance to be shown forth. This loss is the way in to their perception of what his cross has achieved, is achieving and will achieve. They have to be stripped of all false hope and illusory security before they are ready for the resurrection, which is in their lives the final uprooting, the re-routing of them into the way of Christ as opposed to the botched and blind discipleship of Jesus' earthly ministry.

> *Christus innocens Patri*
> *Reconciliavit peccatores.*
> (Christ the innocent one
> has reconciled sinners to the Father.)[7]

These weak men discover through their loss that the risen Jesus has marked them out as special agents of that reconciliation.

Poles apart from the claustrophobic records of merely psychic phenomena, the New Testament breathes perception of a mysteriously but categorically new and liberated world in the making. Central to this conviction of newly transformed life emerging from the melting-pot, from the created chaos over which broods the Holy Spirit of God, is the first disciples' awareness of the remaking of the crucified one in a transfigured life signalled by the empty tomb, shown forth in the manifestations of Jesus risen from the dead, and confirmed in the re-directing of their own lives in the power of the Holy Spirit.

4

Permission to Flee

'My soul is sorrowful even unto death,' said Jesus on entering Gethsemane. Mark's Gospel stresses the dismay and horror which came upon him at that time. It is unlikely to be suggested that his friends were unaffected by his condition, however little they understood it. They saw their master in the throes of an inner turmoil so intense that he sweated blood, and they had every reason to think that this torment of soul was but the prelude to a full course of suffering. In any case they could hardly have been indifferent to the unconcealed intensity of his pain.

Is it possible to say much more than this about the disciples' states of mind during and after Jesus' passion? At first glance the material available appears unpromising. It has become customary to say that the Gospels are not works of biography or of history; and while there are good grounds for treating this assertion with great reserve, they are clearly not psychological case-histories either of Jesus or of his followers. Despite this it is surprising how much that relates to our question can be gleaned from the texts.

The Last Supper begins on a warning note: 'I have greatly desired to eat this passover with you *before I suffer*; for I say to you that I will eat of it no more, until it has been fulfilled in the kingdom of God.' Not even Peter contests the predictive note here, the strong shadow of impending cataclysm. The apostles find themselves caught up in something ineluctable, a destiny devastating in the sense that while it cannot be grasped it equally cannot be denied or shrugged aside. What they come up against is something quite beyond them and yet part of them, something which involves them in their deepest identity whether they like it or not. They have come far too far already with Jesus for them to be capable of detachment.

The complexity of their involvement with him is brought home by the course the evening takes. 'One of you is to betray me,' says Jesus, and the reaction to this disturbing pronouncement is immediate and revealing: 'Is it I, Lord?' asks one after another. If all but one are convinced of their innocence, as the pietistic version of this episode would suggest, then the eleven are merely being slavish in asking this question, giving the master an opening to make clear their innocence. But these men are already experiencing very mixed feelings, not the least of which is fear. If Jesus is to suffer, what about them? His startling announcement brings out all their confusion and weakness, and so they know themselves capable, each in his own way, of betrayal. In the nature of the case they have no notion what is now being expected of them and consequently whether they are ready or able to rise to that expectation. They are made aware by Jesus' statement how thin the line is between their present distress and fright and actual betrayal, should certain circumstances arise. They know themselves as unequal to what is happening, and very liable to concentrate on their own interests at the expense of others, including even their master.

In other words, each detects the seeds of betrayal in his own heart. Each recognizes that he is not single-minded in his allegiance to Jesus, however sincere. Their attitude to Jesus remains ambivalent, and because there is no neutrality they are all potential betrayers. Judas differs from them only in that in him the betrayer is full-grown. It falls to him to enact the evil which is in all their hearts. 'Will I betray you?' is a question which would only be asked if the possibility is real to the questioner:

'. . . deep in all is the base collaborator.
The betrayer is ever oneself, never another.
All must say, 'Lord, is it I?' There is always
Evil in Goodness, lust in love, dust on the dove's foot,

And without it purity's groundless. And the Cross
Had never been.'[1]

It is worth adding here that whenever a death is envisaged, the
future is unknown in a peculiarly sharp and total way. Not
knowing what will be asked of us, we cannot form any judgment
as to how we will respond. Fear of the unknown plays its part,
opening up the conscious possibility of some form of betrayal.

Jesus does not allow the tension of this phase of the
conversation to slacken prematurely. Instead of answering,
'No' as each questions him he says, 'It is one of the Twelve, one
who is dipping into the same dish with me.' He thus focusses
their minds more insistently on the truth that the betrayal
comes from among the chosen, from themselves. Only then
does it emerge that Judas is the man who will body forth full-
grown that evil of which no man but Jesus is free. John adds
that none of those present really understood the significance of
this identification, so that the whole episode has about it an
unrelieved tautness. Jesus the sinless one alone knows what the
stakes are, while the others cannot know, and remain prey to
self-doubt and 'horrible imaginings', than which, as Macbeth
says, 'present fears are less'.

The deeper issues of the interchange thus remain unresolved.
But the immediate tension slackens with the departure of Judas
into the night. The eleven are free to disport themselves
momentarily in a very different kind of imagining which
pinpoints the ambivalence already mentioned: 'A dispute arose
also between them about which should be reckoned the
greatest.'[2] There is a convincing banality about this sudden
change of mood. Deeply disturbed by the surfacing of the theme
of betrayal, with all its resonance for each, they seek relief in a
fatuous argument over status: 'What am I getting out of this
kingdom business?' What could be more natural than to escape
into such an argument? Had this been a sensitivity training
group equipped with a professional observer, the group would
no doubt have been pointedly asked why they had abruptly
changed the subject. Jesus, not bound by the conventions of
such an exercise, takes up their theme in order to bring them

back to reality.

Showing that their starting-point is false, he points out that they have no claim to any status except insofar as they have his spirit of service and have 'stood by me faithfully in my trials'. There is irony in this emphasis when they are at their most benighted and least likely to be true to him. There has to be irony, for in approaching the crisis they are still deep in fantasies. Although they have glimpsed the coming catastrophe and their own incoherence, they have not been able to dwell on or take the measure of these things. Labouring with such a tormenting preoccupation, they have slid off into idle and misplaced speculation, like lost children whistling to keep their courage up, while in the real world the drama proceeds rapidly towards its dénouement.

Suddenly Jesus' tone changes as he addresses himself bluntly to Peter: 'Simon, Simon! Satan, you must know, has got his wish to sift you all like wheat.'[3] Thus Jesus increases the pressure on them, making clear how tenuous as yet are their links with him which they, and Peter in particular, take for granted as being unbreakable. They are told that they are in Satan's grip already, quite without strength in themselves. Jesus spells out for these wretched men what they had already begun to suspect: they are not to be let off the hook of their irresolution, but are to be more deeply caught in its consequences. Only on the other side of this sifting, and by virtue of what he is, not what they are, will they recover or 'come to themselves'. Against such an assault from the master on his cherished image of himself as faithful Peter is characteristically driven to protest too much, only to be categorically informed of his imminent threefold denial.

As if this were not enough, there now comes a final exchange which can only have left the harrowed eleven punch-drunk, 'He said to them, "When I sent you out without purse or haversack or sandals, were you short of anything?" "No," they said. He said to them, "But now if you have a purse, take it; if you have a haversack, do the same; if you have no sword, sell your cloak and buy one, because I tell you these words of scripture have to be fulfilled in me: He let himself be taken for a criminal. Yes, what scripture says about me is even now reaching its fulfilment." "Lord," they said, "there are two swords here now." He said to them, "That is enough!"'

The good time in the sense in which they understood it is already over, their dream of the world at their feet already destroyed by the onset of the powers of darkness. Without the visible and tangible companionship of Jesus they will encounter hostility and rejection. Whether or not Jesus commends the possession of arms for self-defence, the imagery of swords conveys the sense that they will not survive if they continue as innocently unvigilant as they have hitherto been. Nothing will ever be the same again. Unnerved by this shift of perspective, they can only take Jesus' images of their coming conflict over-literally. They draw his attention to their two pathetic swords, at which Jesus impatiently ends the conversation with the words, 'That is enough!' His need to alert them to the struggle in prospect even at the risk of their misunderstanding underlines again the variety and contradiction of the elements in play in their minds.

They have not yet encountered their own or other people's sin deeply enough for the issue to be clear to them. They cannot grasp that the future will be so rough that no human agency other than the crucified victim has the slightest relevance to their predicament. From their point of view, if Jesus does not mean a sword fight, what *does* he mean? What can he mean? His abruptness gives them no answer, and in the garden anxiety takes them over, stunning them into sleep at this least appropriate moment. They can't take it; they can't plumb the depths of the Lord's agony any more than Peter, James and John could scale the heights of his glory in the Transfiguration, that other and contrasting moment when escapist sleep had crept upon them in the presence of too much reality. Jesus now offers them no comfort, only a rebuke and the injunction to 'Watch and pray, lest you enter into temptation.' At last they have to take responsibility for themselves and for their own actions.

Their grief is the shaking of their foundations. Jesus as they have thus far known him, their prop and their stay, their sure anchor, is being removed from them without even a fight. Although they will live to fight another day, and with quite different weapons, that future is a closed book to them. They are engulfed in darkness, with the final humiliation, according to John, of being virtually dismissed from the scene of action by Jesus' request to his captors to let them go. At the level of routine consciousness a crisis is always easier to handle if there is a clear task to be accomplished. It is made clear to the stricken apostles that there is nothing they can do, no role for them at their master's crisis. While at one level it was no doubt a relief to be as it were given permission to flee, they were left nowhere, all the preoccupations touched upon in this chapter remaining to be worked through or dealt with.

5

Peter

The last chapter dealt in largely general terms with the conflicting thoughts and feelings suggested by the Gospels as having pre-occupied the apostles at the Last Supper and in Gethsemane. All the evidence is that they were bewildered and sad beyond measure, without any clear holding-ground or recognizable perspective on what was happening, as they fled from Jesus' arrest. No more is heard of them until Easter, with the notable exceptions of Peter and John, the case of Peter being of particular interest.

Lord Hailsham has suggested that in dubbing the jelly-like Simon 'the Rock' Jesus was making a joke.[1] This is entirely probable, though hardly the whole story. The normal picture of Peter as an impulsive coward does scant justice to his role in the New Testament, although his blunders are undeniably writ large. What is worthy of future comment from the point of view of this book is the treatment he received from Jesus.

With Peter Jesus never, it seems, pulled any punches. While this makes good sense as part of the preparation of Peter for his role as confirmer of his brethren's faith, this very rough handling needs to be borne in mind in any consideration of Peter's behaviour after Jesus' arrest. Peter had the unique and unenviable distinction of having been addressed by Jesus as 'Satan', a name never lightly or idly used in the New Testament. He had also been upbraided by Jesus for his doubt when walking on the water. He was roundly told at the Supper, against his own vehement protestations of loyalty, that he would thrice deny his Lord. To cap it all his intervention to protect Jesus from arrest is met with a very curt dismissal: 'Put

your sword back in its scabbard; am I not to drink the cup that
my Father has given me?' Peter's gesture is not merely spurned
but condemned as an attempted obstruction of the Father's will
and purpose for Jesus. His intervention is thrown back in his
face by these words and by the immediate healing of the man he
had wounded. A wretched state of affairs in what Peter sees as
his last encounter with Jesus; for his next move is to follow after
the arresting party 'to see the end'. This flat phrase, not used of
John who accompanied him and whose perspective is mysteriously different, suggests the hollow finality in Peter's mind and
heart. He cannot get Jesus sufficiently out of his hair to be able
to withdraw from the scene at this stage, but he knows that the
Lord has gone beyond him.

   The denials which follow, if seen in the light of his stormy
relationship with Jesus culminating in the knock-out blow in
the garden, are open to a less moralistic and more interesting
interpretation than a bout of cowardice. In any case it is largely
on the fact of these denials that Peter's reputation for cowardice
is based, but this way of understanding them is at odds with
much other evidence. A coward does not set out to walk on the
water; nor does he declare his faith in a most unlikely Messiah
whose popularity is on the wane, as Peter unequivocally did
against the odds at Cesarea Philippi. When Jesus asked on that
occasion: 'Will you also go away?' Peter replied: 'Lord, to
whom shall we go? You have the words of eternal life.' Nor
would a coward take the ludicrous risk of attacking a well-
armed party when his own group has only two swords, still less
enter the High Priest's palace just after cutting off his servant's
ear in the presence of others now in the palace. If Peter's denials
arose from cowardice there is a weird discontinuity in his
behaviour which, while conceivable in theory, should not be
immediately preferred to a more economical and inclusive
explanation.

   In Gethsemane Peter has been chastened and humiliated by
Jesus at the moment when he would have most wished to help:
after all, the Lord had said not a moment earlier that swords
were now in order, were indeed a priority. This seemingly final
rebuff tore Peter apart, so that even while being drawn to see

the end he felt deeply alienated from Jesus, whom he no longer wished to know. The denial of Jesus is not a lie but an expression of Peter's immediate reality, an outburst emerging from the swirl of contradictions within himself. He found his rebuff too much to bear, coming as it did on top of the spiralling pressure of the situation around Jesus. His own inadequacy was no doubt present to him, though still opaque. But had not Jesus also let *him* down, and much more drastically, by arousing expectations which he had, after the initial stages of his ministry, signally failed to fulfil? He had built up Peter in particular, but to what end? Only a deepening gloom, an oppression of spirit, climaxed by the lowering prediction of Satan's sifting which, he had been led to suppose, he could not avoid; and that final, magisterial dismissal. He no longer knew this impossible man,[2] and said so to his questioner with rising vehemence issuing in a curse.

It is normal to resent someone whom you feel has let you down with a bump, and still more someone who has virtually told you that you are useless and then abandoned you to your own devices. Why should Peter, from his own point of view, continue to take it on the chin? Beyond this, and deeper, is the peculiarly intense resentment always felt towards a person whom you have let down. Peter would not have been human had he not resented the person who by being the occasion of his failure had revealed to himself his own weakness. It is perhaps tendentious to affirm these reactions of Peter, but to do so makes fuller sense of the depth of his denial and of his bitter sorrow than does the idea of panic. Peter had had moments of panic before; this reaction during Jesus' passion is surely something more total, the expression of a genuine rejection of Jesus or at least of a profound division within himself which gave Satan a foothold enabling the sifting of Peter to proceed.

There is another and complementary way of looking at Peter's denial. Peter was dominated by Jesus in a way which was as yet in some aspects childish. He needed to grow out of this infantile form of dependence if he was to be any good to himself and others, if he was to become the rock which Jesus said he was. While Jesus understood Peter, it was not possible for Peter to understand Jesus if he continued to cling to this dependence. When Jesus said at the Supper, 'Where I am going you cannot come,' Peter absolutely refused to accept what he was told, and strove to dictate the situation: 'Why can't I follow you now? I will lay down my life for you.' Jesus treated this as wishful thinking and immediately broached Peter's imminent denials. The mere departure of Jesus would not in itself have broken this spell had Peter not, in that abrupt and seemingly uncompassionate going, discovered himself as separate, as someone much more complex, much more in need of redemption, than his childish self-image as the faithful and all-loving disciple would suggest. He had to face and be brought through his alienation into sorrow. The cock-crow jolts him into looking the facts in the face. Jesus knew best, but Peter had to find this out for himself. The tradition that Jesus caught Peter's glance at that moment is appropriate, as Peter begins to see himself and Jesus with fresh eyes.

6

The Beloved
Disciple Remembers

The more the author of the Fourth Gospel perceives the mysterious grandeur of Christ, the more he perceives the scope of the historical and concrete event . . . In this Gospel the mystical imperiously invokes the historical. There is no divorce between them. Their solidarity is the keynote of the Gospel. (F. J. Leenhardt).[1]

This and the remaining chapters of Part II will pursue themes touched upon in the passion and resurrection narratives of the Fourth Gospel. To clear the ground it will help to summarize those points conducive to my argument which have considerable scholarly support. Readers unacquainted with the world of New Testament scholarship must not fear that they are about to be lost in a morass of abstruse technicalities. In any case this exegetical excursus will be very brief.

In the first place reputable scholars[2] hold that the themes of the Last Supper discourses in John were taken from the *private* teaching of Jesus. Such scholarship would also support the notion that these themes were being dwelt upon at the onset of the final crisis. Apart from the psychological plausibility of this, the other Gospels record a similar emphasis at the time when Jesus' situation became overtly critical.

A third corroborative point from the scholars comes in the suggestion that what we have in the Johannine discourses is an *interpretation* of Jesus' sayings rather than an attempt at a verbatim account. Thus some at least of the sayings were clearly well-established before being put to use in John, while there would in any case be an *a priori* probability of some authentic source. Workers in the field have drawn attention to the way in which Johannine themes correspond to things reported more briefly by other evangelists.

So much for what is widely agreed. A further claim which carries no such consensus must now be strongly pressed: that the Johannine discourses represent a particular perspective on the passion which goes back to a historical reminiscence. I am aware that I am breaking new ground here in an area of very great uncertainty.

In this connection one single but not uncommon mistake needs to be exposed: the notion that if a tale is rounded and well-told it is thereby shown to be untrue. The Johannine discourses, clearly having been polished and worked over, are always liable to strictures of this kind. Yet in reality the likelihood that some of the insights may have taken a long time to come to the surface does not contradict the view that such insights were implicit in what was remembered from the beginning. This point, which obviously has all sorts of ramifications beyond the Johannine tradition, will receive more extended treatment in the chapters on memory in Part III. In the meantime, it is worth noting that reluctance to accept this may spring partly from a naive notion of the availability from the past of the bare facts of particular episodes. The assumption would be that it is possible, or at least in principle desirable, to disentangle fact from interpretation in any given narrative. My understanding of memory would imply that such a working assumption merely renders the story – any story – incoherent. It might be added that to think *at all*, even about present experience, in terms of 'the bare facts' is already to falsify the relationship between the knower and what is known; but it would be inappropriate to follow that thought any further. Without more delay we can now turn to what the Fourth Gospel has to tell us.

All four Gospels show the disciples as subject to a sense of distancing and helplessness in relation to Jesus during the Supper and, most markedly, in Gethsemane. But in John there is also in play a deeper dimension, which finds a striking correspondence in the experience of being with someone who is very close to death. Remember that John alone of the eleven witnessed from close at hand the events in the High Priest's palace, and subsequently Jesus' ordeal and death on the cross. It is therefore no accident that in John's account of the Supper the theme of going away is given a strong, positive stress. In particular the emphasis of the reported interchange between Thomas and Jesus on this subject implies that John had already, unlike Thomas, begun to grasp that Jesus' departure would turn out to be a blessing for all concerned.

To Thomas at the Supper Jesus says that where he is going his friends cannot come; those who are dying often communicate a similar though far less articulate sense of entering realms not yet available to the witnesses. Everyone feels distanced as the person advances on the journey into death. In the words of someone bereaved, the dying person seems to grow away from us, 'as if we were already in different realms, with different holding-points, different terms of reference'.[3]

While this awareness of a distance opening up may involve strain, it can also be a revelation if we are ready to be receptive rather than imposing our own thought-patterns or assumptions upon what is happening. It can even become very difficult to leave the bedside of a dying person because one is learning so much, being enriched. This perspective would perhaps become more widespread if we could rid ourselves of the odd assumption that it must be sheerly negative to be dying. In its turn this notion is probably a rationalization of the inability to face our own death. I should hazard the generalization that we have more to learn from those very near to death than they have from us, at least where there is a living faith. The distancing and powerlessness already mentioned can indicate and promote release from the hitherto existing contours of the relationship, so that a deeper reality of sharing can begin to be revealed, however inarticulately.

An example is provided by Henri Nouwen's reflections on the time spent at the bedside of his dying mother, when she was very restless but beyond verbal communication:

I felt powerless, small and helpless, but also peaceful, strong and quiet. I was seeing and feeling something I had never seen or felt before, an experience that to be described would require words that have not yet been found: Powerless yet strong, sad yet peaceful, broken yet whole . . . Everything was truthful, there was no lie . . . We experienced the privilege of being close to her suffering, intimately connected with her pain . . . I have never felt so strongly that the truth can make us free.[4]

In other words, what is at one level a distancing is in fact a deepening, an initiation into a different level of reality and relationship. What now unites the dying and their friends is not so much their relationship in itself as their sharing in the mystery, their being drawn together into that which encompasses, unites and upholds them in and through their shared weakness and pain. Another's journey into death, which seems to separate, is in reality a strengthening of the 'survivors', a redisposition of them in relation to the mystery of life through death. This can be adequately appreciated only when you have been touched by the radiation of peaceful strength which can come from or pass through someone who is dying. The Holy Spirit, we might almost say, is extremely reluctant to miss such opportunities to foster newness of life in the surprised openness of the bereaved.

This, I maintain, is the perspective of John. He is the one for whom the distancing of Jesus during the passion is already a revelation. This is confirmed by two episodes, one at the foot of the cross, the other at the empty tomb. The dying Jesus gave his mother into John's care, and commended John to her motherhood. John was able to provide human continuity, as is proved by what happened, in being a son to Mary: 'From that hour he took her into his own keeping.' Then at the tomb it was John who believed. It is not said that John believed *because* the tomb was empty; the suggestion is rather that seeing the emptiness of the tomb enabled things to fall into place for him.

Some of those who decry the empty tomb claim that it was the appearances of the risen Lord that were decisive for the apostles. This is to forget or to discard the Johannine testimony. The resurrection narratives tell of the empty tomb and the appearances: they cannot be dismembered without a degree of distortion. John believed at the empty tomb: if this sits uneasily with one's notion of the resurrection it hardly solves the problem to abolish the tomb.[5]

It is scarcely odd to find very different attitudes among the disciples: given that the relationship of each to Jesus was different, it follows that the bereavement experience of each was different. The same death is known in a whole spectrum of diverse ways by those most closely involved. There is no reason why this should not have been as true of Jesus' death as it clearly is of other deaths. Nor should any contradiction be supposed between the various ways of being connected with the same death. Peter, John and Thomas have their place, and nobody is morally superior. Jesus did not exempt John from his dire prophecy: 'You will all be scandalized this night because of me.' This is perfectly compatible with the idea that John hung on to more of the Lord's words, or hung on to those words with more of himself, than did the others: in other words that initially Jesus' perception was more successfully shared with John than with the rest.

Having reflected on 'how it was for John', we can now look in more general terms at perspectives suggested by the Johannine version of the Last Supper. In claiming so much for John I do not mean to imply that the other disciples saw absolutely nothing of what he saw. That it is not a question of 'all or nothing' should become clear in the remainder of this chapter.

The exalted tone and content of John's account of the Last Supper stands in striking contrast with the synoptics, but the stress on the disciples' incomprehension is every bit as strong. Their interjections, always very brief, serve as foils to the unfolding of Jesus' reflections, each question or statement from one of them eliciting a further phase of the Master's discourse. It seems best to read John as complementary to the other evangelists, his absorption in the mind of Jesus adding another dimension to their more spare accounts of the conversation which took place that evening.

While the range and exaltation of Jesus' words in John's version might appear to render irrelevant any questions about his follower's dispositions, it needs to be stressed that John goes to great lengths to make explicit the elements of conscious preparation for the passion which Jesus wished to express. The Lord was not speaking in a vacuum, but deliberately and exhaustively preparing the eleven for his death. The last discourse makes little or no sense if read as a speech to nobody in particular, or to a sheerly uncomprehending audience.

It follows that the idea that the disciples understood nothing, which I have so far emphasized, requires clarification and radical qualification. Without crediting Jesus with an omniscient human consciousness we can reasonably suppose that if he 'knew what is in man' he would have known well enough that his friends would not immediately understand and hold in the forefront of their minds everything he needed to tell them, or that they needed to hear, that evening. He also knew that the kernel was what was happening to him, so that if he could keep the focus insistently on his passion they would be disposed for understanding. All were in crisis; in crises the human mind tends at some levels to become intensely receptive. It is as if a new faculty or type of receptivity, or a remarkably speeded-up version of the old, comes into play. This heightened awareness is deeply disturbing because it is out of rhythm with life's 'normal' tempo and with the rest of one's being.

The revelation thus encountered at a critical moment takes time to assimilate, time to become a personalized and fully appropriated part of the recipient. Many things are grasped, or at least glimpsed intuitively, which have not yet come to full consciousness. I remember clearly that when a doctor once told me that a close friend was certifiable and intermittently suicidal he was not telling me anything I did not already know with a part of myself: I already had the evidence, and could read the signs. It was evening when this doctor pronounced, and the substance of what he said had been staring me in the face throughout an anxious day. It nevertheless took much longer for this picture and its implications to form a shape in my mind in coherent relation to past, present and future. The doctor's statement was a step on the way towards reality, but even after it I knew and yet did not know, for I was labouring with something which could not be fully taken in without the shattering of many of my categories for the interpretation of reality.

In images of the present, of the immediate future and of the longer term Jesus gave the disciples a framework of meaning which would be enspirited and enfleshed for them when they ceased to be trapped in their own confusion and dismay. He communicated to them that there was something of decisive significance *to be understood* about his passion, whatever their present desolation. He told them that these seemingly doom-laden events had an inner thrust and shape quite other than they might suppose: this hour of darkness had the true form not of a dead end but of an initiation.

A humble parallel is the teaching of Shakespeare to school-children, sometimes opposed by educationalists on the ground that the poet's work is beyond their range of experience, hopelessly remote from their present mental world and there-fore incommunicable. Better, according to some educationa-lists, to encourage them to study local manhole covers.[6] Such views tend to be self-justifying, for a teacher who thinks thus is not likely to have much stomach for *Hamlet* or *Twelfth Night* in the classroom.

A two-pronged reply can be sustained: part of the purpose of communication is to broaden horizons and deepen perception, to draw the pupil out into larger worlds of meaning beyond his immediate boundaries, to dispose him for new experience. The second prong is that there is already much more to build on than the view I am attacking would suggest: there is already a good deal in common between Shakespeare and a group of modern adolescents, despite surface appearances. The conflicts caused by jealousy, ambition and frustrated passion; the seeming triumph of malice and self-seeking; the durability of true love and fidelity in and through tragedy: there will be at least some understanding for some. For these at least, what they take in at the time will be a starting-point for fuller perception in the years to come. This was my experience in being plunged into *King Lear* and *The Tempest* virtually unaided by the literary critics. A rich fund of imagery and incipient perception arose; while there was much that I did not understand, and much else that I glimpsed very inadequately, none of it has subsequently been without point. I should not wish to have lacked this enriching formation.

This, I suggest, was the case with the disciples and Jesus' last discourse, with the difference that what was at stake was total, urgent and dependent upon specific future events for its full comprehension. The communication is indivisibly one of words and imminent events – neither made sense without the other. But Jesus' words, and their reception of his words at some level of their being, are all-important. No event convinces entirely of itself, without any interpretative context. Jesus' words, albeit in a highly mysterious way, supply just such a context, directly engaging with the presuppositions of his friends' desolation and challenging their inmost hearts.

These men to whom the risen Lord appeared and to whom the Holy Spirit came in the beginnings of the church were weak and obtuse in all sorts of ways, but by no means *tabulae rasae*, by no means unchanged by all that had gone before, especially Jesus' preparation of them for their mission. It will not even do to describe their behaviour immediately after Jesus' arrest as simply aberrant, for what could or should they have done? Their flight does not prove that they had taken nothing on board from the Lord's discourse: under such stress they could hardly have held his words in their conscious minds with any continuity of concentration. It does not follow that the discourse was already as if it had never been uttered. It was submerged rather than lost: ready to be re-activated, to re-emerge and to grow into its true proportions in connection with the unfolding of events from Calvary through Easter to Pentecost and beyond. In the midst of so much muddle, at the height of evil's onset, there was a purifying and clarifying power in the single-minded, passionate, almost ruthless focussing of Jesus' words upon his going, in human terms the end but in reality the reconstitution of humanity, a new definition of man in relation to God in the incipient renewal of all creation.

'Now at last they know,' said Jesus to the Father, 'that all you have given me comes indeed from you', thus showing that the new perspective, the truth of the matter, has already made great headway in the hearts and minds of the eleven. This change in them, Jesus seems to be saying, is irreversible though as yet incomplete. This new perspective, this revelation, this newly-born faith will only be overshadowed, not cast out, by their subsequent doubts and fears. A deceptively frail-seeming seed has already germinated within them, in time for the coming of the hour of the powers of darkness. At the Supper Jesus ensures that the seed is firmly rooted, leaving the rest to the Father and the Spirit's nurturing.

In considering the disciples' relationship with Jesus the role of understanding in the sense of precise and exhaustive analysis should not be over-stressed. It is commonly assumed that it is impossible effectively to sustain a relationship with another person without understanding what makes that person tick. The deepest corrective of this notion I have heard was spoken by a friend: 'You shouldn't think you *can* understand. What makes the difference is to accept that there is something *to be understood*,' i.e. to respect and accept without reservation the other person's reality, to remain open to that abiding mystery in the conviction that love and truth will prevail. This is opposed to a straining to know on the instant what the other is all about, and thus seeking to confine the mystery within one's own categories.

The disciples did not need a clear and comprehensive notion of 'what made Jesus tick' in order to love him and to become his faithful followers. 'You have the words of eternal life' is very different from 'We understand every word you say.' 'This man speaks with authority' is not the same as 'We know what this man is about'. T. S. Eliot's suggestion that poetry can communicate without being understood is applicable to many other forms of human discourse. Within the confines of a cosmos still only partially transformed the other's meaning can in any case never be fully grasped.

How wearisome it is when the ostensibly interested observer says to the believer: 'You tell me exactly what this is all about so that I may decide whether or not to sign on.'

7

Orphaning, Judgment and Glorification

At the Last Supper, particularly as reported by John, Jesus was deeply pre-occupied with his relationship with the Father and with the Twelve. His concern is that they will not be left as orphans: note the implication that if their relationship with him were to come to a final end, so would their relationship with the Father. He does not doubt that their relationship with him is and will remain the decisive factor, while his own relationship with the Father is at the centre of the gathering storm: Jesus' anguished prayer in Gethsemane, and his cry of abandonment on the cross, confirm this last point with searing clarity and maximum economy of words. Nor does Jesus guarantee them against the experience of being orphaned, for that is precisely what will happen to them; the point is that he will not *leave* them orphans, but will come to them. They are, then, to be orphaned for a time; and this image in the mouth of one whose intimacy with the Father was so close, so consciously constitutive of his whole being, suggests an unimaginably total desolation.

Yet, says Jesus, this desolation is expedient for them. On this basis he proceeds to spell out the meaning of his death in five ways. This chapter deals with the first three, while the fourth and fifth ways each need a separate chapter. For the outline of these ways I am indebted to Yorick Spiegel.[1]

First, it is only in his going that they will come to see his true significance. Only thus will the Holy Spirit come, to bring to their minds all his words and enable them to grasp the shape and purport of those words and of his whole life. It is only after his death that his friends will be able to recognize who he is. There is here an exact parallel with the evidence of many bereaved people that it is only after the beloved's death that he or she is perceived in his or her true stature, without the distortion hitherto caused by transient factors. This is worlds apart from the wishful thinking of 'only seeing the good' in the dead person. It is a genuine re-orientation which illuminates that person's most positive and therefore abiding qualities without denying the reality, for what it was worth, of the inadequacies and faults. These last no longer matter because they are seen to have lost their power to bind the deceased and, indirectly, the bereaved: having played their crucifying part they have exhausted their reality and no longer exist.

The true direction and intent of the dead person's life is now shown forth to the survivor, stripped of ephemeral clutter, which except at privileged moments tended to obscure the truth. In addition there is an element of domination in all relationships, which is removed or at least lessened in bereavement. Jesus is saying that his death is the way in to his friends' growth in freedom of spirit, including a true evaluation of Jesus himself without that clinging dependence on their part which put him in a dominating role. Remember Peter's extreme resistance to the Lord's desire to wash his feet.

In other words, if the disciples' relationship with Jesus is to become what it truly is, if it is to be fully realized and enacted in their lives, then he must leave them. Only thus will they see him in proper proportion and be enabled to follow his way and spread his word. The Spirit will not come unless he goes, and without the Spirit they will remain hamstrung; blind and unfree, not capable of taking responsibility in his name. One meaning of the biblical phrase 'in his name' is 'in his presence': the renewed presence of Jesus after the orphaning is not in doubt. This presence, recognizable in the enabling power of the Spirit, will reveal his true role in their lives and in the life of mankind: he will be seen as their way, and our way, to the Father. Equally he will be seen as the Father's way with them, something which they could never grasp in his pre-crucified life because they were too dominated by the immediate situation.

To this extent their earlier fidelity to him, real enough as far as it went, was muddled, and muddied by their own unfreedom and unseeing. His going and their orphaning began to clear the picture, or to give birth to quite another picture.

The second of the five ways in which Jesus according to John expresses the meaning of his own death is in terms of judgment, a function of the Spirit, of whom Jesus says: 'And when he comes, he will convince the world of sin and righteousness and judgment.'

Jesus' death facilitates the Spirit's coming by putting or leaving everything in the melting-pot, rendering his friends uniquely vulnerable, exposed on all fronts to 'the slings and arrows of outrageous fortune': he leaves them adrift in a world without hope. Yet by that very fact, viewed in connection with their relationship to him, his death begins to open them up to the action of the Spirit by leaving each alone with himself.

In parallel with the view of 'the wound of bereavement' already expounded, Jesus' death is not in itself their problem: it merely faces each one of them with the problem of himself, exposing their long-standing irresolution and inadequacy, already to some degree overt and yet masked by the form their relationship with Jesus had hitherto taken. On the other hand they have already come too far with him, they have already learned from him too much about themselves, other people and their world, for them to be able to conclude without remainder that everything that had gone before was simply in vain. They are faced with a conundrum of a severely practical nature which they experience as an impossibility: where do we go from here?

Jesus says they have to go through the pain of this impossibility if they are to receive the Spirit, who will empower them for right judgment. It is in and through these men that the Spirit's work of convincing the world will proceed. Jesus' death prepares the disciples accurately to discern the power of sin at work in the world, and correspondingly to recognize by the Spirit's power his own righteousness. They will come to see clearly and believe whole-heartedly that Jesus was right all along; that their doubts, confusions and fears were without foundation in him but projections of their own weakness and sinfulness. They will see that the world's failure to recognize him and desire to be rid of him were the fruit of sin.

Furthermore, Jesus' death will dispose the disciples to see that the world is already judged. This is not a matter of Jesus having to die in order to ensure that they will duly come to agree with him and act accordingly. What they need to recognize and acknowledge is the fact that his crucifixion *is* God's judgment on the world, 'a judgment which takes the form of resurrection'.[2] This judgment is not a denial of sin but a declaration of forgiveness. Jesus' death is the definitive judgment on the world: the bringing of this person to this extremity revealed the world as under the reign of sin. At the same time this death brought that reign to an end in the loving enactment of God's forgiveness. In the light of the resurrection, then, the cross at once judges the world as sinful and declares its forgiveness.

There is something so critical and so profound here that words fail, but there is again a remarkable degree of convergence with the witness of the bereaved. In this life everyone is judged to some extent by the standards of this world: this judgment and its consequences are crucifying, not least in that the judgment reacts upon and influences the person who is judged, especially when the judgment is made by an otherwise faithful and loving person. Each carries his or her burden of inner conflict, which is intensified by this-worldly judgments from others. The bereaved person comes to see himself as in his degree a crucifier of the beloved who has died. Far from being morbid, this is an accurate insight, beyond moralistic blame, into what was the case. The picture of the departed one as a victim of the spirit of this world comes to occupy a central place in the bereaved's consciousness. This insight into one's own crucifying role gradually expands into an awareness that we are all victims in this sense as well as crucifiers, but the definitive image of the victim is the departed one, in whose case the image can truthfully achieve some completeness, a sense of a consummation through victimhood.

In stressing the link between his death and the coming of the

judging Spirit, Jesus shows that this judgment is not for
condemnation. It is the power to discern the true victimhood,
initially of Jesus himself and potentially thereby of all mankind.
So in the deceased the bereaved person comes to perceive
beneath the overlay of conditioning and habit in both partners
the seed of self-giving which was that person, and how that seed
grew through suffering to become all that matters about the
'lost' one. 'The light shone in the darkness, and the darkness
was not able to overcome it.' In the short run, which from an
ordinary human perspective may appear as a very long run,
there is no question of the light casting out the darkness, which
is a testing and purifying of the light.

Until the crucifixion the disciples had only glimmerings of
the scale and role of the darkness which was at once the world's
and their own. Only in living through that 'hour of darkness'
which snuffed out the life-spark could they be brought to
themselves in the realization that the end was in truth the
beginning, and that the acknowledged hopelessness of their
plight was rich soil for the Spirit's cultivation. They had to be
convicted of sin by being plunged into darkness before they
could discern what was really happening, namely that their
sins were nailed to the cross with Christ. Their sins no longer
had power to bind them, not least in their relationship with and
view of Jesus himself. They had not literally killed him, but they
had been scandalized because of him.

Thus it could be revealed to them who this man really was:
the saving victim whom they had helped by their defaulting to
crucify. The risen Lord bore the wounds of his passion. In thus
judging themselves in relation to Jesus they have no difficulty in
judging the world in his regard, with his eyes. Mark's Gospel in
particular lays great stress throughout Jesus' ministry on the
failure of his followers either to understand or to respond
appropriately. Jesus' last discourse, in contrast but not in
contradiction, earnestly commends to the Father their fidelity,
which in the event prepares them to acknowledge the world's
sin, the rejection of Jesus. They know themselves as having
been strengthened and enriched in and through their failure-
riddled fidelity to Jesus, whom when the Spirit comes they are

therefore in a position to glorify in much more than a purely commemorative sense. In the resurrection encounters they know themselves as henceforward 'in the world, but not of it'.

This remembering is a new kind of judgment which penetrates to who Jesus was, is and will be in relation to the Father and to all that is created. His reality is no longer filtered through the fractured mirror of their small-minded expectations and unconscious fears. Now Jesus is seen and declared as the victim of the 'ruler of this world', the fullness of his boundless love only now being revealed to them: 'Having loved his own, Jesus loved them to the end.' That is what he was really doing when they wondered whether he was leading them to disaster, or seeking to take them further than they could go: he was loving them to the end in the face of odds which at the time they could not assess.

We have already trespassed on the third way in which Jesus declares his death's meaning: it is through his death that he will be glorified. As already hinted in a number of ways, such glorification is by no means alien to, still less contradictory of, other witnesses. In and after the death of a loved person he or she is often remembered in a wholly unromantic fashion. This way of remembering takes the focus off the ramshackle bundle of this-worldly preoccupations and limitations in terms of which much of the relationship was formerly conducted. In true remembering nothing of the past is falsified or merely obliterated. Everything is reinterpreted as the bereaved person is progressively set free from those elements of guilt and hatred which he now sees as having held him in a clamp.

To do justice to this aspect of bereavement the word 'memory' becomes strained almost to breaking point, unless its fullest sense of active comprehension as an enhancement of life in the present can be brought into play. Any narrower concept of memory will not work in this connection, as P. J. Kavanagh indicates in the following thoughts centred on his dead wife:

To turn her into a memory would be impossible, there are some persons, some events, it isn't possible to shrink in this way; they're outside our range.

I have felt her presence so powerfully at times that I've found it easy to believe a great many things. The sky would not have held all the things I could believe. It comes, it goes, it will come again, and it leaves a residue. Once you've experienced the infinite significance of another person's life you feel something of the same for all lives, and for your own. There remains in the world this infinite significance and to every event we owe a responsibility.[3]

It may seem churlish to suggest that it is because Kavanagh defines memory too narrowly that he is forced to reject the word. The fact remains that in biblical terms the concept of memory would easily carry all the resonances of his compelling story. Kavanagh avoids the pitfalls of either uncritically exalting his wife into a figure of hagiography or 'realistically' diminishing her by negative analysis.

Two further references may help to eludicate this concept of memory and the associated process of glorification. The Richard whom I have already quoted writes, like Kavanagh, about his dead wife: 'Only after her death do I see the depth of *what was really there*, obscured by the human limitations, tensions, conflicts, seemingly self-destroying and other-destroying.' Linking this with T. F. Torrance's view, in *Space, Time and Resurrection*,[4] that the resurrection revealed *who Jesus was all along*, it seems that the seeing of Jesus as he really was could come about only after those involved had worked through a misapprehension similar to that referred to in Richard's last phrase, 'seemingly self-destroying and other-destroying'. Or at least the seeing itself would have to reckon with and deal with such a misapprehension in his friends.

Jesus was sinless in a world ruled by sin, a world dominated by evil until his death. He engaged this evil at its heart, challenging it to do its worst. Despite what has been said about their fidelity to Jesus, his friends were not yet free of the spirit of this world – they were not without sin. To the extent that this was so, misunderstandings and distortions of Jesus were inevitable, for they could see nothing quite straight. There is reason to suppose, at times at least, and especially towards the end, that they inclined to see him as embarked on a self-destructive course which was liable to be also their destruction. The way in which he approached his arrest, and the attitude to it which he sought to instil into them, did not inspire any immediate confidence that the situation was in hand.

This theme, already discussed in the chapter on Peter, has wider applications. The Emmaus story makes the point most graphically in its hollow sense of abject failure and disappointment: 'We had hoped . . .' The news of the empty tomb and the angel's message could not crack open this constricted consciousness which defined Jesus as a failure and all their hopes as vain. There is no suggestion of further questions arising; they are gossiping and grumbling, glumly cutting their losses as they sum up to one another and then to the stranger the disaster as they see it. True enough, there is no overt criticism of Jesus on this occasion; but there is an intense sense of being let down, of being radically disappointed on the very brink of freedom – of being in effect sold a pup by their allegiance to Jesus.

It is he who takes the initiative, guiding them patiently through the scriptures. His reply is in effect: 'Don't you know who I am? Don't you know who I was? Can't you see what has really been happening?' Thus he draws them out of their false version of him and of his history even before they recognize him. 'Did not our hearts burn within us as he talked to us upon the road?' is the key to the story, for here in the very depths of their wretchedness is the change of heart which prepares them to recognize the risen Lord at the eucharistic meal he shares with them.[5] From then on, through their healed remembrance of him, he can be glorified.

8

Seeing Again

The fourth element in Jesus' anticipation of what his death means is that his faithful ones will see him again:

> I will not leave you orphans;
> I will come back to you.
> In a short time the world will no longer see me;
> but you will see me. . .
> In a short time you will no longer see me,
> and then a short time later you will see me again.

It is best to treat the resurrection appearances as an initiation into that fuller union with Jesus sealed and sustained by the Holy Spirit after the appearances cease. Nevertheless the appearances are crucial, as are the parallel but more limited phenomena found in other bereavements.

The evangelists are at pains to stress the difficulty the disciples had in coming to terms with the appearances. These manifestations of Jesus in his new way of being were not readily acceptable to them. Far from being already convinced by faith that all was well with him they were, at times at least, confused and frightened in his risen presence. He had to work hard to convince them of his reality and of his further purpose for them. Some effort of imagination is needed to get behind the pietistic and artistic accretions of subsequent ages which so easily deprive these events of their cutting edge. There is a temptation to picture the appearances as blandly comforting. Yet if the passion was a dereliction, the appearances are the beginning of a reorientation which is extremely costly from the point of view of their existing assumptions.

A group of people darkly struggling to make sense of their loss of Jesus are now newly and radically challenged. They have lost him in his death: their cherished Messiah, their protector, he who was going to restore the kingdom to Israel and give them positions of honour, he who would enable them to beat the world at its own power-game. They have lost the Jesus of their fantasies, but the Jesus who finds them in his resurrection presents them with their true task of witness and service in showing them his reality as crucified saviour. Many scripture scholars who are embarrassed by the resurrection stories seem blind to the extraordinary tension involved in this new form of encounter with Jesus. The risen Lord speaks the word of peace to his chosen ones, but this is a peace 'not as the world gives', a new kind of peace free of illusion and wishful thinking. Far from being a sop, a dubious short-circuiting of unbelief, the appearances are a challenge to faith.

The scandal of the cross is not abolished by the resurrection but elevated to the status of a mystery:[1] the appearances present the disciples more acutely than ever with the question of who Jesus was. They have to reopen the question of the meaning of their involvement with this man who has newly found them in his death. The New Testament taken as a whole against the background of the Old is the answer to that question. The scale of the further conversion of heart required and initiated by the resurrection appearances should not be underestimated. The two disciples on the Emmaus road did not recognize Jesus even when their hearts burned within them as he expounded the scriptures. When Jesus appeared on the lakeside the disciples were afraid to ask him who he was: although they knew it was the Lord, they could not bring themselves to have the identification confirmed. This is perhaps the most compelling instance of their difficulty with the appearances: if this was indeed the Lord, mysteriously but unmistakably present to them after his death, what was being asked of them? So alien was this manifestation of Jesus to whatever was still unredeemed in them that it seemed safer not to acknowledge him.

Thomas, more straightforwardly, was in a state of doubt, a

chronic condition[2] rather than a moment of uncertainty. Thomas wanted to believe but protected himself against the threatening nature of that desire by holding himself in a self-contained posture in the face of his friends' witness. He may even have been jealous of them for having shared a critical moment which he had missed: 'This can't have been real, for I wasn't there.' In any case his response to their story was in a tone of low-key agression: 'I'm not going to be sucked in to this new excitement. If this is the real thing I shall believe only if I see directly and immediately for myself.' The New Testament evidence was falsified by those theologians of the 1960s who sought to reassure such people by saying that those aspects of Christianity which most deeply challenged them were unworthy of belief. Thus was established a false peace in which the doubter could continue to cling to his doubts. The crisis was postponed. Theological argument was beside the point. What Thomas needed, and duly received, was the healing touch of the Lord's wounds, which set him free to worship. We have good cause to be grateful to Thomas.

The 'seeing again' reported by the evangelists is extremely disconcerting: it is the offer of a new and most uncomfortable kind of peace in following the way of the cross. It is not the restoration of former security in the Lord's companionship, but a confirmation that such security was an illusion, definitively exposed as such by the crucifixion. In this particular God's judgment and the world's coincide: no way back. If the crucifixion is seen as in one aspect the world's judgment on God, the resurrection appearances reveal that same crucifixion as God's judgment on the world. This judgment shows that the only life the world can recognize is far from being the whole story. Jesus said at the Last Supper that the world would not see him again; but this unseeing could not obliterate or render insignificant what the disciples saw.

The evangelists show no concern with the 'how' of the resurrection, and little with the precise nature of the appearances. But the notable restraint of their narratives suggests a presence of a different order from Jesus' way of being during his ministry. 'Do not cling to me' on the one hand, but on the other 'a ghost has no flesh and bones as you can see I have'. It is fashionable to stress the credulity of the apostolic age in the area of what is now called the paranormal, so it is well to remember that both resuscitated corpses and ghosts were not beyond the ken of that generation. It was in an age which took such phenomomena seriously but was perfectly capable of making the appropriate distinctions that the disciples proclaimed Jesus' resurrection as an unprecedented and transforming event. While this proclamation was made in the light of and on the basis of having seen Jesus again, they did not say: 'You all know what happened to Lazarus, and to the widow's son at Nain. Now the same thing has happened to Jesus!'

This mysterious presence of Jesus to his followers had two purposes: first, to convince them that he had been raised from the dead; secondly, to prepare them for their new ministry. Some scripture scholars emphasize the second purpose almost to the exclusion of the first, as if the role of faith would be undermined had the risen Lord appeared in order to prove his resurrection. Yet such an exclusive stress on the commissioning aspect of the appearances[3] is at odds with the Gospel narratives, which strongly suggest that if the disciples' relationship with Jesus is to issue in authentic mission they must first come to terms with his risen presence. When Jesus said to Thomas: 'You believe because you can see me. Happy are those who have not seen and yet believe,' he did not thereby challenge the genuineness of Thomas' belief, based as it was on 'seeing'. He pointed out in these words that others would come to believe through the apostles' witness.

There is no conflict between the kind of seeing recounted by the evangelists and true believing. Thomas touched the risen Lord, Mary Magadalen clung to him, and some of the disciples ate and drank with him. Deeply offensive to the spirit of this world, these stories and others show the foundational role of the appearances in the growth of apostolic faith, while also emphasizing that as such their part is transitional. Transitional, not expendable: 'They are important because they bring us the conviction that the person we have loved is . . . alive in a timeless reality.' Thus Stephen Verney, interpreting in the same breath the resurrection appearances and the experiences of himself and his children after his wife's untimely death: 'Things which belong in time, and things which belong outside time, are trying to express themselves through the same events. They happen in clock time, but they are also timeless.'[4]

Linking this heightened awareness with bereavement, Verney places the resurrection appearances firmly in the setting of the relationship between the bereaved and the deceased, showing that through the opening-up of this relationship wider perspectives come into play: '. . . when somebody you love has died, the barrier between these two worlds grows very thin, and a new pattern of events is set free to happen around us.' The notion of Jesus' death as the setting free of mankind, which emerged from what happened to the disciples after the crucifixion, finds a very powerful resonance here. The cross was regarded not merely as a setting free from evil but as a setting free to love, to be forgiven and to forgive.

The disciples, confirmed by the appearances in their relationship with Jesus, themselves became the centre of a new pattern of events from Pentecost onwards. They did not see this pattern as their own doing but as a gift, the work of the Holy Spirit in giving them a new kind of life springing from and linking them most intimately with Jesus in his return to the Father. According to Verney the appearances 'have to give way to something more important still, which is the experience that we, too, can come alive and be with them (i.e. the deceased) now, in that same reality beyond time'. These words offer a balanced assessment of the role of 'seeing again' both in the lives of the disciples of Jesus and in subsequent bereavement.

The appearances of the risen Jesus are not themselves the resurrection: contrary to what a narrowly rationalistic strand in Christian apologetics would have us think, they are not the knock-down argument against the sceptic. They are rather an assurance to his chosen ones that the Lord has been raised, an assurance which is itself a summons to enter into that fullness of life about to be available to them. The message of the risen Jesus is one of forgiveness for all men: but for his followers to accept and promulgate this message they have first to accept his healing, reconciling presence. They need to claim initially for themselves the forgiveness now offered to them by this Jesus whom they have in their diverse ways denied: the appearances are an appeal to accept on their own behalf the fruits of his anguished labour of love for all mankind. 'Love your neighbour as yourself': to do this effectively they need to know themselves forgiven, themselves accepted at their worst, themselves healed of the consequences of the ambivalent attitudes outlined in earlier chapters. In their seeing of him again their sense of having betrayed Jesus, and of having been let down by him, in other words their self-hatred, is thus exorcised.

The complexity of their intimate involvement with him left them with a need to see him again, and he for his saving purposes needed to show himself to them. Here again it is the relationship which gives shape and coherence to these mani-festations of his risen being. Like other bereaved people, Jesus' friends needed to perceive and adjust to the reality of the person who has just died if they were to avoid being locked in the past at the price of new possibilities of life. Sometimes bereaved people come under great stress through a refusal to deny the element of 'seeing again' in the face of others who for a variety of perfectly understandable reasons devalue their testimony, explicitly or otherwise. 'There is nothing spooky about these appearances,' writes Verney: 'They are absolutely natural – so natural one might call them "supernatural".' They cannot be adequately described as illusions, for such bereaved people are quite aware that they are seeing the dead person in a new mode of presence.

This is a most delicate matter, for it is not possible to deny what has been seen without betrayal. If those around the bereaved reject, evade, or belittle their testimony they may begin to mistake their 'seeing' for the whole truth, as a desperate alternative to agreeing with the world's judgment that they are deluded. This mistake is the 'clinging' from which Jesus vigorously deterred Mary Magdalen before it could become habitual. Stephen Verney reflects:

We have to stop clinging – to stop clinging to the person we

have loved – because we can never be together again in this
world of space and time. We have to let them go, and this is
the hardest and most painful thing of all, because it means
letting go the whole pattern and structure in which we have
existed . . .

Here we see that the way of resurrection is a way of risk, for in
the very truth of the appearances lurks a danger of mistaking
them for the whole reality, the final possession of the deceased.
'The nigher you are to truth the nigher you are to error,' wrote
Dame Julian of Norwich;[5] and in no aspect of man's quest is
this more apt than in bereavement.

It is therefore hardly surprising that immediately after the
last 'seeing' the Book of Acts records that Jesus' closest friends
and relatives entered on a sort of retreat, going at once to the
upper room where they joined in continuous prayer. Something
absolutely decisive has happened. There is no going back, but
as yet no going forward either. They need time to assimilate
what has occurred, and the gift of the Spirit to discern the full
dimensions, purpose and power of this happening. Even at the
last appearance of Jesus the eleven were still fussing fruitlessly
over the possible consequences of what was going on: 'Lord,
has the time come? Are you going to restore the kingdom to
Israel?' As so often before, Jesus' reply made clear that they
were asking the wrong question. In a sense he is not going to do
anything, and certainly not the kind of thing they are still
expecting. He put the ball firmly in their court by drawing
attention to the future role of the Holy Spirit, and to their own
missionary task in the Spirit's power, not just in familiar terrain
but 'indeed to the ends of the earth'.

The chosen ones had to be conformed to the mind of the risen
Jesus *after* the period of 'seeing again'. It is of deep interest here
that in Acts Luke is at pains to name the small company who
waited in the upper room in prayerful expectation: the eleven,
Jesus' closest women friends, his mother and his close relatives.
All the people who had been in continuous close contact with
him over long periods of time; all those who most needed to be
shown the Spirit's truth for themselves, while others, just as

genuinely but less intimately caught up in his fate, could be expected to accept the witness of these people. The presence of the relatives rings true, for their earlier hostility, or perhaps desire to save him from himself, is indicative of abiding concern of a kind quite normal within families; a concern much deeper than being ruled either by affection or by dislike, and often only made conscious by bereavement.

'Gradually,' writes Stephen Verney, 'we begin to find that there is a new structure holding us fast, and a new pattern where our true selves are coming alive, in a timeless present, together with the person who has died and the risen Christ.' Here the resurrection of Jesus is seen as decisive for all bereavement. It is the risen Jesus who shows forth, initially in the appearances and subsequently in the power of the Spirit, the meaning of the disciples' bereavement, which therefore encompasses and patterns all bereavement. Yet for Verney it is his own and his children's loss which brings this truth to life: for him, 'Do not cling to me' is of the essence, meaning, 'If you cling to me as I was, then I cannot be with you now as I am. If you cling to me as your teacher – as an authority outside yourself – then my truth cannot become your truth, which springs out of the depths of your own heart.' Right to the end of the period of the appearances the disciples continued to lean on Jesus precisely as an authority outside themselves. His parting words made clear that the onus henceforward would be on them. Only at this point did the resurrection cease to be a purely domestic issue.

According to Yorick Spiegel, it is a long-term feature of bereavement that the dead person is not abandoned or forgotten. 'But the form of his presence has changed; it no longer is bound to his personal appearance, which dissolves in the memory just as does his body. He becomes a possession, never to be lost, by being restored within the bereaved.'[6] A possession not in the sense of a private asset clung to in the interests of the bereaved person's self-securing against the unknown or against others, but as a gift which is to be shared. This inexhaustible possession carries with it a proper self-possession, an opening of the true self to new opportunities, a re-charging and re-directing of immense energies. In the language of psychology, the dead person has been interiorized or incorporated in the bereaved. The phrase 'the body of Christ' applied to the company of believers could hardly be more appropriate. If the deceased has been incorporated in the survivor, the matter can with equal truth be stated the other way round: the survivors have been incorporated in the one who has left them. Jesus is for all: it is the availability of life in him which the apostles preached when they proclaimed the resurrection. He had become so intimately and firmly present to them that he was beyond seeing.

This is by no means to undervalue the seeing which occurred, but rather to place it as a stage in the deepening of their relationship with him, a phase of their conversion to his truth and life, a sign of his possession of them as much as theirs of him. The presence which they saw was not backward-looking, seeking to tie them to repetitious re-runs of the limited life and sharing of the years of his ministry. This particular seeing is only intelligible in terms of the uniquely total crisis reached in their relationship with Jesus at his death; that crisis in its turn could only be understood in the light of who Jesus was, and by whom he was sent. In his book *Christology at the Crossroads* Jon Sobrino[7] writes: 'Only with the appearances of the risen Jesus do the disciples see that God's ultimate word is love rather than condemnation. They realize that what happened to Jesus is the destiny of all human beings.'

9
Joy

I have told you this
so that my own joy may be in you
and your joy be complete . . .
I shall see you again, and your hearts will be full of joy,
and that joy no one shall take from you . . .
While still in the world I say these things
to share my joy with them to the full . . .

Joy is not commonly associated with death. It is here that Jesus'
attitude to his death is most forcefully at odds with the spirit of
this world, which sees death as final negativity. Death in the
world's eyes is that which destroys relationships and thus
defeats man's best endeavours to establish and sustain a
community of love, whether in family life or in a wider sense.

This fifth and final theme in Jesus' preparation of his friends
for his death is therefore the most paradoxical. If this perspective can be hoisted in, the world is really stood on its head. The
joy of which Jesus speaks is linked with 'seeing again' but is not
coterminous with it; the seeing initiates the joy, but it is the joy
which abides as something 'no man shall take from you'. Their
joy is Jesus' own – 'my joy' – able to be communicated to them
in a timeless way after his death. In other words it is a joy in
relationship, a stable sharing in his relationship with the
Father, as is shown by the concluding words of Jesus' prayer to
the Father at the Last Supper: '. . . so that the love with which
you loved me may be in them, and so that I may be in them.'

Jesus declares that the disciples will have an abiding joy in
consequence of his death, a joy in the light of which their

immediate grief will be as nothing. Yet the intensity of their sorrow is emphasized rather than minimized by his words, which acknowledge it as wholly appropriate to the rending of their companionship with him. None of the Gospels plays down the disruption involved here, which is writ large in the starkness of all the passion narratives. Jesus' going is un-equivocally the end in terms of everything they have so far seen and anticipated. There is not a word to suggest that their grief is something they have any power to alleviate, much less get over. No counsel of the stiff upper lip, but rather an affirmation and an entering into their anguish. It might almost be said that Jesus encourages them to grieve while they need to, while there is good reason to do so, for he knows that it is only by walking down that tunnel that they will come upon and be surprised by the joy which lies ahead.

The word of future joy is therefore not designed to diminish that sorrow which is the fitting response to their loss of him, but only to suggest that the end of the story is not desolation. This joy will give meaning to their grief, just as the birth of a child gives meaning to the mother's pain in childbirth. The suffering of the disintegration of one form of relationship is seen to be no more than the price paid for entry into a new and more comprehensive mode of relationship.

Was the disciples' bereavement unique in this sense? Is the theme of joy the point of divergence between their bereavement and all others? Superficially it would seem so, for joy is not an obvious keynote of bereavement as we know it. The difficulty here is similar to the problem already touched upon in some cases of 'seeing again'. Joy clashes even more spectacularly with the world's idea of death, and therefore with the common expectation of what happens in bereavement. In particular, any sign of joy at such a time is liable to be seen as lack of respect and affection for the person who has died. These words of Jesus are appropriate : 'Unless you become as little children you shall not enter into the kingdom of heaven.' For the child grief and joy are very close companions, each being entered into with like seriousness as occasion offers. This whole-hearted spontaneity of response to what happens tends to become blunted in adult life, as the 'cares of this world' obtrude and burgeon into all manner of unproductive anxieties, not least a ruling concern with what other people might think or will think.

Joy in bereavement is not socially acceptable. It is shallow and unhistorical to imagine that this is a feature peculiar to the modern world: the apostles at Pentecost, preaching in exaltation a crucified man, were thought to be drunk. This earthy 'explanation' of their condition is matched in more sophisticated terminology when any sign of joy on the part of the bereaved is described as unbalanced or, quaintly enough, as morbid. Yet the fact is that joy in bereavement is by no means uncommon. Since beginning this study I have been amazed by the range and amount of evidence to this effect. The witnesses are too numerous and their circumstances too diverse for them to be lightly dismissed as exceptional cases.

Joy is not an alternative to grief as a response to bereavement. There is an interaction between the two which does not conform to any neat pattern of joy succeeding sorrow as the end-point of the process. Spiegel[1] over-simplifies here: 'That a grief process, like the death of Jesus, can *end* in joy appears hardly comprehensible to the person suffering the loss; it can only be described as a result understood later' (my italics). That understanding comes later is undeniable; but to suggest that joy succeeds to grief in orderly sequence is to constrict the kaleidoscopic nature of what happens to bereaved people. Joy is often experienced as a kind of concomitant of grief from a very early stage. This joy does not remain in the same form, and may even appear fleeting or at least unpredictable in its coming and going. But it leaves what P. J. Kavanagh[2] calls a residue: there is about it something irreversible, a definitive movement of the heart beyond the sense of sheer loss which is most people's unexamined image of bereavement. Even if this joy becomes overlaid by a new onset of anxiety, fear or guilt it abides at a deeper level as a reference-point, a sacramental initiation into a phase of deeper life and sharing with the deceased person and with others.

Such joy can be most insidiously threatened by guilt. Some

bereaved people are put under considerable pressure by their fellow-Christians' disapproval of manifestations of joy. The spirit of this world, rarely entirely absent from Christian attitudes, insists that the bereaved should be sad and be seen to be sad. In the preparation for and the enactment of a funeral peculiarly intense tension can arise if joy is shown by the nearest and dearest. In such circumstances it is not unknown for offence to be taken by other mourners. Yet St Paul commends a specific attitude to the deaths of Christians: 'You are not to lament over them as the heathen do, with no hope by which to live.' This is not a prohibition of mourning as such, but of hopeless grieving. Lamentation cannot be the essence of bereavement for anyone who knows the risen Jesus as the firstborn of many brethren. Paul's emphasis here is seen in perspective if it is remembered that he was not given to putting restraints on the expression of wholesome grief at human partings.

There is no question of insensitivity to an appropriate sorrow and its due expression. The point that mourning is necessary is poignantly made by the behaviour of the birds in an early and little-known poem by W. B. Yeats, 'The Ballad of Father O'Hart'.[3] Father John was an exceptionally devoted priest in Ireland in the penal days. He was much loved by all – people, animals, birds:

> The birds, for he opened their cages
> As he went up and down;
> And he said with a smile, 'Have peace now'.

The flaw was that he saw no need for ritualized mourning:

> He bade them give over their keening;
> For he was a man of books.

When he died at the age of ninety-four the people wept but observed his ban on keening. Not so the birds!

> There was no human keening:
> The birds from Knocknarea
> And the world round Knocknashee
> Came keening in that day.

The young birds and old birds
Came flying, heavy and sad;
Keening in from Tiraragh,
Keening from Ballinafad;
Keening from Inishmurray,
Nor stayed for bite or sup;
This way were all reproved
Who dig old customs up.

It is perhaps the interplay of grief and joy which makes
bereavement so bewildering, rather than either the joy or the
grief considered in isolation. Both intense and total, the onset of
one or the other or of a mysterious combination is so
unpremeditated as to call all previous bearings in question. In
this sense Spiegel is right to stress that understanding comes
later, as a new pattern of life begins to take shape in the
bereaved person. Only then is the joy fully recognized as an
abiding quality of life, come what may. The resurrection
appearances brought joy to the disciples, but there was also
anxiety, which persisted in the form of questioning: 'Lord, has
the time come? Are you going to restore the kingdom to Israel?'
Only at Pentecost, fifty days after the crucifixion, is this
confusion and anxiety dissolved.

The joy with which we are concerned solves no problems but
transcends all difficulties, convinced that no problem is ultimate in the light of the resurrection of Jesus: 'I have come that
they may have life, and have it more abundantly' (John 10.10).
'Grief,' writes Spiegel, 'can become an experience that leaves a
human life not more deprived but enriched and can result in a
deeper understanding of the deceased and the bereaved.'[4] I
would add that this enrichment comes to be known in the
deceased as well as in the bereaved. Indeed the latter's sense of
personal enrichment is experienced as a by-product or consequence of the transformation of the beloved, of his or her being
set free to be henceforward a vessel of sheer praise and glory. This
glimpse of an aspect of the communion of saints sees the 'lost' one
both as personally transformed and as able in consequence to
communicate something of this transformation to the 'survivor'.

In the Johannine discourse it is not the seeing again but the joy which Jesus says will last for ever. The implication is that the seeing will be enough to initiate in his disciples a joy which no man can take from them, a joy which cannot be snuffed out by the spirit of this world. This joy is of such a kind as not to need continuous seeing for its continued vitality. The seeing is transient, but the joy abides as an irrefutable earnest of the fullness of relationship which will come only at the end, when in Paul's words, 'We shall know as we are known'.

The seeing of the risen Jesus recorded in the Gospels is a showing forth of God's love in him, but *for them*, a showing of that love as available to them in being conformed to him, to his heart and mind. In becoming thus universalized, Jesus does not cease to be personal but is perceived as personal more fully than before, as the centre and heart of God's affair with mankind. Again, continued seeing is not necessary to sustain this perception and would, it is suggested by the Lord's words, prove a barrier to coming into possession of the full implications of the seeing itself: 'Do not cling to me.'

The joy begun by this seeing is not self-contained, not a purely interior and individualistic consolation, nor yet merely a sort of domestic bonus for the ingroup or a sectarian asset. It is a radiation the essence of which is to be shared, to be communicated to all men everywhere. It takes time to assimilate the true nature and dimensions of this joy: indeed this cannot be adequately done until the second coming. In the meantime it takes the coming of the Holy Spirit at Pentecost to launch the missionary implications of this joy, to bring the disciples to an active realization that this is the kind of joy it is – contagious or nothing.

Likewise with the bereaved person who can withstand the assault from within and without on his inexplicable joy: it is experienced as outgoing, as propelling him or her towards new relationships and into hitherto unsuspected depths in existing relationships. Such joy is always known as a gift to be given, like all the fruits of the Holy Spirit. There is not necessarily any external drama in this showing; but there is an unmistakable delicacy and serenity about its manifestations. A funeral can give vibrant expression to this, and does so more often than is commonly realized. Its reverberations can have such quiet power that people on the fringe of the occasion who come with no very developed expectations are deeply touched.

On the other hand it is in the nature of the case that joy in bereavement does not have the same dimensions as the joy of the first Whitsun. This was the birth of the church as the body of Christ, while each bereavement is a step in the building-up or completion of that body. Pentecost makes no sense without the disciples' bereavement, but no subsequent bereavement makes sense without Pentecost. The disciples' bereavement is decisive for the whole destiny of mankind, while every other bereavement contributes in due measure to the outworking of that destiny. There is only one bereavement in the course of which the deceased is proclaimed as Lord and Saviour, as the Son of Man and the Son of God. There is only one bereavement during which the deceased is encountered and acknowledged as having power to forgive all sin and to bind up all wounds. All other bereavements make a more limited but no less real claim.

It will be appropriate to end this chapter with perhaps the most provocative reference to joy in the entire New Testament. At the beginning of Hebrews 12 the author says that Jesus endured the cross 'for the joy that was set before him', and exhorts Christians to a similar attitude. It would be hard to think of any passage which more effectively and concisely undercuts all attempts to interpret Jesus' death merely moralistically. Far from being a bonus not consciously sought, joy is here presented as the motive for the passion, although this motive does not exclude others given elsewhere.

The role of faith is not diminished by putting joy at the centre, for it is faith which gives the assurance that there is joy ahead. Faith, as the same author writes, is 'the substance of the things to be hoped for', and primary among these things according to this letter is joy. A joy anticipated in faith is quite different from a purely imaginary joy, for it resonates with a joy already intermittently experienced. The New Testament lends no support to those Christians who think of this life as essentially 'this vale of tears',[5] for it takes present suffering too joyfully for that.

Part Three

IO

Neither Martyr nor Suicide

Belief in the divinity of Jesus arose in and through the disciples' bereavement. More precisely, it results from the totality of their experience of him, of their relationship with him. Theologians, like all experts, love to dissect, but the point is missed if any moment or phase of this relationship is scrutinized in isolation. In his lively and pertinent book *The Easter Jesus*, Gerald O'Collins SJ[1] draws attention to the tendency among theologians to absorb the resurrection 'backwards' or 'forwards'. In the former case the resurrection is as it were collapsed backwards into either the incarnation or the ministry of Jesus or Good Friday. Sometimes it is the incarnation which is seen as *the* saving event, sometimes the teaching and example of Jesus; for some theologians the resurrection is not a further event beyond the crucifixion. The collapsing of the resurrection forwards occurs when the dominant consideration is its resonance in the present; or when the future coming of Christ so fills the picture that time, history, evil and suffering are devalued.

In thus resolutely opposing all tendencies to deprive the resurrection of Jesus of its absolutely central place, O'Collins might have added that all such emphases also involve some distortion of the other mysteries, or aspects of redemption, into which the resurrection is thus absorbed. These various facets can only be integrated when we grasp the centrality[2] of the crucifixion and resurrection in the disciples' consciousness. The structure of that centrality can in its turn only be appreciated from the point of view of how they experienced and related to Jesus at each stage of their contact with him. If we have to single out an event it must of course be the resurrection. Yet the resurrection as they knew it was in part a commentary on and illumination of all that had gone before. At the risk of labouring the obvious it is worth asking, for instance, what the resurrection would have been without the Galilaean ministry. What place could it have found within their scheme of things? More pertinently, how could it have established in their hearts and minds a new scheme of things of a kind to which the concept of re-interpretation is but a weak approximation?

My concern is not to prove the divinity of Jesus but to show this belief as born of what he was in relation to them, a relationship which from the point of view of all that had gone before foundered catastrophically in his passion. He had brought the kingdom of God among them and had pointed that kingdom out into the whole world of humankind. He had categorically identified the kingdom with himself in the sense of his life in relation to the Father and to all men. Despite his followers' incomprehension they were enabled to go along with him, to stay with him as the vehicle of life, of meaning, of Godwardness. There was no precedent for such a ministry, for such a life as he lived out amongst them and for them, although Israel had had its share of prophets, wonder-workers, outstanding and unforgettable leaders and teachers. Jesus was for the disciples the nearness of God.

No precedent, then, for his whole way of being amongst them and for them, for the kind of sharing he had with them. In the next phase, the preparation for the passion, the lack of precedent is even more apparent. No trace here of the dignified resignation of the pagan hero or philosopher who calmly faced death as the ineluctable consequence of the rightness of his cause.[3] Death broods over the Last Supper as an alien force, a dark shadow. We are in a different world here from the four-square, intransigent fidelity of, for instance, the Maccabean martyrs. For them the issue was straightforward: to compromise or not. They could see the fittingness of their deaths. By contrast, death simply did not fit with the sense of boundless life which Jesus possessed and had begun to share. It was felt by him and by his closest followers to be in searing contradiction with that pure freshness of life which was his.

It was thus as an act of sheer obedience[4] that Jesus' death came over the horizon, not as an appropriate climax to his ministry. For the sinless man, conscious of his intimacy with the Father, death, the wages of sin, could not be fitting, still less be seen as such. To him at this point of anticipation it was the obedience, not the death, which was appropriate, as his intense inner struggle in Gethsemane makes clear. Insofar as his death was the Father's will it must be expedient for his followers, and, ultimately, for all mankind: but for Jesus himself it was horrifically, unimaginably unfitting. In a chapter on prayer in *The Brink of Mystery* Austin Farrer reflects: 'When Christ prayed at Gethsemane, he began from where he was, with his natural horror of an unspeakable ordeal. It was in praying that he found and embraced the saving will.'[5]

In his study of Jesus' knowledge Raymond Brown claims that there is no hard evidence for postulating in Jesus any psychological development of knowledge about his future after the beginning of his ministry.[6] This conclusion is reached by way of meticulous scrutiny of the texts used by other scholars to support the contrary thesis. If Brown is right, the place of Jesus' death in his own heart and mind becomes extraordinarily mysterious. There is an important sense in which his death cannot really come into focus, so alien is it to his sense of life and mission. All that he can see is that this death is being demanded of him by the call of an ultimate and inexplicable obedience to his loving Father. We cannot imagine such a demand being made, still less being complied with, for we have no analogue for Jesus' intimacy with the Father, and therefore none for his existential predicament.

The Gospels portray Jesus as hearing and heeding this call: 'Not as I will but as thou wilt.' According to Hebrews he 'learned obedience by suffering'; while St Paul says that he 'became obedient unto death'. Even St John, who tells us that 'Jesus, having loved his own, loved them to the end', does not say that he died directly for love of them. While there is no question of denying love as the motive of his obedience, it is the mutual love of Father and Son which is primary, and so constitutive of his obedience. While in principle there can be no separation, still less contradiction, between this foundational love and his love for his chosen ones, it is as if part of his ordeal was the onset of a seeming disconnection between the respective demands of these two loves: 'You will all be scandalized this night because of me.' During his ministry Jesus had already drawn attention to the dire fate in store for the bringer of scandal to little ones: 'Better for that man that a mill-stone should be tied about his neck . . .' Now, as his passion looms, he sees himself about to become the cause of scandal to his chosen and beloved disciples. The New Testament treatment of Jesus' death is consistently and conspicuously free from any tinge of romanticism, sentimentality or heroism. The language of these modalities was clearly found hopelessly unsuitable to handle this incomparable combination of life-affirmation with an obedience which seemed to undermine Jesus' very being.

Jesus did not befriend death as Don Juan did, but endured it. This is the most overwhelming aspect of the gospel story, showing Jesus engaging on and accomplishing a course of suffering quite beyond any available morality. Nothing short of a divine obedience, an obedience from God to God, could justify so monstrous a course, involving the end of his mission and the sifting of his disciples by Satan. 'I have come to do the will of my Father, who is in heaven.' In thus obeying his Father's will Jesus did not doubt that the meaning of his destiny would be revealed; but it was in abandonment and alienation even from the Father, and as a conscious stumbling-block to his loved ones, that he finally committed himself into the Father's hands, unconsoled by the limpid wholeness of perception characteristic of his ministry.

Jesus, it would seem, was uniquely exposed to evil. He had, by virtue of his intimacy with the Father, which is a positive way of expressing his sinlessness, a uniquely unambiguous encounter with evil at work in this world. This is a clue to the peculiar desolation of his end both for him and for his followers, however little or much they may have consciously grasped.

Those who had come to regard him as possessed of 'the words of eternal life' now saw him as succumbing to evil on the cross. They could not yet see that only he could thus confront evil by allowing it to have its head, that only he was eligible for such exposure, was able to plumb the depths: 'He descended into hell.'[7]

What of the disciples in the face of such a frame of mind and such a course of action in their Lord and Master? What does his condition have to tell us about their state as the passion proceeded and his death was accomplished? Notice again the striking difference in spirit between the passion narratives and the records of the last hours and moments of other men and women who were publicly executed for their fidelity to identifiable causes. 'A brave man will die in the mornin'; for bein' true to his cause,' as the song in the spoof Western has it. In all these cases there is a holding-ground alike for friend and enemy in the cause itself, though differently interpreted by each. Whatever the rulers of the people thought, there was no cause from the disciples' point of view why Jesus should give himself to death, and every reason why he should not. The fact that in the nature of the case they cannot grapple with his obedience, that they cannot be adequately attuned at this stage to what is happening, cuts them off from him and from each other.

Thomas More, who, in the days of his power, did not scruple to condemn heretics, is nowadays anachronistically pictured as a prisoner of conscience in the modern sense. In reality Master More pondered doubtfully on papal authority for seven years before concluding that he was 'the King's good servant, but God's first', thus finding himself compelled to disobey the King and pay the price for so doing in the Tudor world. More himself, Thomas Cromwell and the king saw the odds and the issue clearly enough. More's refined conscience refused obedience to Henry VIII in the name of what he saw as a higher obedience, the nature of which was in principle sufficiently clear to all concerned. He was sincerely regarded as a purist by some and a rebel, if not a heretic, by others; but the ground on which he stood was comprehensible, if not agreeable.

More's death was of a piece, and seen to be of a piece, with his life. He sought no confrontation, resigning his high office as soon as he realized his conscience was no longer at ease in the King's service. He did not publicize his attitude, nor yet seek a show-down. The sticking-point when it came was not of his choosing, but it was consistent with the development of his thinking. More had no quarrel with his fate, but Jesus had such a quarrel when he wrestled with the Father in Gethsemane and protested his abandonment on the cross. Yet Jesus chose to die in a sense in which More did not; More accepted his death when circumstances presented him with no other alternative to compromise, while Jesus endured death as the consequence of an unexampled obedience. 'He accepted an obedience which brought him to his death', that death which as we have seen was in collision with his life and mission. 'I am come that they may have life, and have it more abundantly' entered into radical tension with 'I have come to do the will of my Father who is in heaven.'

More lay low at the onset of the crisis, but Jesus insisted on putting himself not merely at risk but on a collision course by going up to Jerusalem 'for the feast', a time of maximum excitement and therefore danger. His 'Palm Sunday' procession into the city and his encouragement of Judas to do quickly what he was going to do are in line with this dark insistence. He is not, on the other hand, a Jan Palach, who saw self-destruction as the only coherent response to Russian tanks rolling into Czechoslovakia in 1968, thus provoking Pope Paul VI into a compassionate homily on the moral error of suicide. Jesus, neither a martyr nor a suicide, undoubtedly suffered and died at the hands of other men. Yet in worldly terms there is more of the suicide than of the martyr about him; so much so that the not insensitive script-writers of *Jesus Christ Superstar* were constrained to attribute to Jesus a death-wish.

In Jesus' own mind the initiative is his: he sees himself as laying down his life, not his judges or executioners as taking it from him. They have no such power over him; indeed the accounts read as if the powers that be are there only to afford him the opportunity for his obedience. 'They know not what

they do,' said Jesus of his executioners; and Acts is even more
explicit when it records the prayer of the companions of Peter
and John after their release from arrest: 'In this very city Herod
and Pontius Pilate made an alliance with the pagan nations and
the people of Israel, against your holy servant Jesus whom you
anointed, but only to bring about the very thing that your
hand and counsel had pre-determined should happen', namely
Jesus' death.

It is easy to imagine Jesus and the disciples as unpolitical
pawns in the power game of the wordly wise who know what's
what. This is far removed from the New Testament picture
where Jesus has the initiative and chooses to surrender it,
counselling his friends in an attitude which similarly inverts the
wisdom of this world: 'Be ye wise as serpents and simple as
doves.'

In what other death are the supposed agents of death
categorically recognized by the victim, and before long by his
friends, as unwittingly corroborating the will and purpose of
the loving Father of all mankind? No other superficially
comparable sequence of events furnishes parameters within
which this death can be understood.

> He nothing common did or mean
> Upon that memorable scene,

suggests a nobility of bearing in King Charles I over against his
enemies, the kind of bearing which makes them look 'common'
and 'mean' by comparison. The Gospel narratives give us no
hint of such ambivalent dignity: it is as if Jesus has gone already
far beyond such studied behaviour into a degradation where
there was no beauty nor comeliness in him.

It is Jesus' death, interpreted by his resurrection, which
enables all other self-sacrifice to achieve its full and true
nobility, for no other death is known as having total power to
save. There is no place here for that self-righteousness which
can corrupt people in pursuit of lofty causes, whether justice in
southern Africa or industrial democracy in this country. This
must always be borne in mind if Pilate, the priests and the
people are not to obtrude too much. It was not they but the

disciples who came to know this death as salvation, as forgiveness and as healing.

There can be no question of Jesus' friends having been swept up on the instant into sharing the state of mind and heart which led to his austere act of final obedience; for such a foreshortening, while at first glance neat, ignores the fact that they were left with a contradiction at the heart of their perception of Jesus. He died in final rupture with his cause of life-promotion, as is relentlessly and cogently argued by Jon Sobrino.[8] They, and they alone, were confronted by this contradiction in its absolutely intractable form, although others on the fringe may have glimpsed it. If this contradiction was present to Jesus, how much the more in those who survived him? If they could not then enter into the nature of his obedience, how much more starkly final was the end in their minds? If this man who was for them the nearness of God, the power of God at work amongst them and wholly in their favour, was dead; if his cry to the Father had not been heard; if he had known rejection by the Father in relation to whom his whole being consisted; if he had neither saved himself nor been saved from falling into the void, into that relationlessness[9] of death which traditionally awaited all men; then all was indeed over. I say 'all', not merely an episode, for Jesus had already become in his conscious intention and theirs their life and their way.

Thus for his followers Jesus' death was at this stage much more like a suicide than a martyrdom, although what is most striking is the extent to which even at the time, if the New Testament is to be believed, it came through as neither. This death found in their minds no point of comparison. Jesus' death, like his life only different, was unique.

II

The Poor, Sinners and the Sinless Man

It has already been argued that the deepest level of Jesus' suffering was his sense of the radical unfittingness of his own death, culminating in his conviction of abandonment by the Father at his darkest hour. For this man, the beloved Son, to experience such rejection was a form of suffering not subject to comparison. This point is easily blurred, if not missed, by a pietistic assumption that because he was God *any* suffering on Jesus' part is especially to be wondered at and praised. Apart from the fact that this perhaps unconscious premise obliterates the true dimensions of the passion by collapsing it backwards into the incarnation, humanity is thus cheapened. It is possible to stress the condescension of God towards man, and supremely in becoming man, in such a way that man is diminished.

God did not see himself as condescending in any of these dealings with man, for the whole thing is an act of love. It is man who insists on putting God in the role of he who condescends, for man cannot cope with his own guilt. The point is elegantly and economically made in the prophetic books of the Old Testament, where Israel's God is *a God who is with the poor*. This in its turn can be wrongly taken to mean that it is wonderful that God is ready to stoop from his Olympian height even to the extent of being with the great unwashed. Thus this sublimely beautiful and healing strand of revelation is thinly moralized by guilt-ridden man into saying no more than that God is undoubtedly much better than us who never get round to coping with the obvious surds in our society. It may alleviate guilt a little to imagine that the omnipotent God, who after all is in a position to do something, deigns to care for these wretchedly unlovable people.

Far from being a statement of God's condescension, the conviction that God is with the poor is a definition of God; or, if you prefer, a statement of the kind of God the true and only God is. Our God is a God of compassion, whose nature it is to be with those who are without standing or security in this world's terms. 'Foxes have holes, and the birds of the air have nests, but the Son of Man has nowhere to lay his head.' This redefinition of God, this glimpse of the real nature of God-with-us, thus hints at a redefinition of man, an exaltation of the lowly who are especially chosen of God. Of course we are all in a way poor in God's sight; but our radical poverty has to surface and be embraced if we are to be open to God. Again, and at the risk of wearisome repetition, this is a matter of relationship, and specifically of that comprehensive, ongoing-without-end relationship which is God's affair with man. As Alan Watts would have put it, this is God at play in his cosmic creation:[1] the notion of God at play with man cuts at the roots of our portentous categories of God-thought. In the sight of children rapt in play, or of adults absorbed in the timeless ritual of cricket, we have a potent reflection of the deeper play of love which is our true nature and destiny. Certainly not cat and mouse.

The poor in the biblical sense, the poor of the Lord, are those who for one reason or another have not, or have ceased to, set their sights on any of the securities this world in its unredeemed aspect offers to the unwary. Those whose lives, however wretched their material, intellectual or spiritual circumstances, are not tied down by and built into worldly roles and expectations. 'Watch and pray, that you enter not into temptation': these words were aptly spoken in Gethsemane, when Jesus had just come to terms with the full implication of his own poverty.[2] The maintenance of true poverty requires prayerful vigilance.

The biblical image of the poor, along with the claim that they are especially the place of God, transparent vessels of God's life, breaks open the half-awakened concepts in which God's relationship with humanity is routinely formulated. Lofty metaphysical questions about the nature of God are here raised in the same breath with severely existential questions as to who are the poor. Who is this God whose very being it is to identify himself with the many varieties of the wretched of the earth? Who are these creatures with whom it is God's nature to be thus lovingly involved? The prophetic witness allows no disjunction between these two kinds of question, which are in truth the perennial question addressed by man to God, and finding the inclusive answer in the crucified Jesus whom God raised from the dead as the first-fruits of the new creation. If the poor are God's place, his special abode on earth, they are the place *par excellence* of man's openness to God. Being poor, then, is a condition of freedom from this-worldly constraints which is a receptivity to God. When Jesus shocked the moralists by declaring, 'The poor you have always with you', he might well have had this sense of the word in mind. Mankind needs the poor, not as a surd but as his blessed opening to God.

If the poor are rigidly identified with those who sleep out under the bridges of Paris or London, with the unjustly oppressed peoples of South Africa or parts of South America, or even with the starving in the streets of Calcutta, the cutting edge both of the prophetic message and of the gospel is caricatured either into sentimental fatalism, or, more destructively, into strident moralism which, denying its own impotence, then finds a negative outlet in hatred of the oppressor. I once asked an interested friend whether Western European opponents of the present South African régime ever found it in their hearts to pray for the leaders of that government. This candid friend replied that he felt rebuked by the question, going on to explain that armchair liberals could not afford the possibility that such people might be redeemed; if they did the whole structure of their approach to the issue would collapse. In such a mental world support for the oppressed can only be sustained by reducing the oppressor to chronic and incurable inhumanity.

These tortuous caricatures of charity play no part in the thinking of the remarkable Mother Teresa of Calcutta, who has said that whatever the suffering of the people she serves, there is a deeper anguish in the mental torment of very many in the affluent West. In reaction to the prevalent Western tendency to romanticize and moralize her achievement, she affirms her work with a truly Christian sense of proportion as being, hopefully, a drop in the ocean of all the works of love which come from God and proceed in this world.

It was counted against Jesus that he consorted with notorious sinners. All men are sinners. As friend of sinners Jesus was the friend of all, but he reserved his special attention for those whose lives were at a turning point and whose need was therefore most acute. Remember the encounter with the rich young man: 'Jesus, looking upon him, loved him.' Remember Nicodemus, a leader of the people, who came to Jesus by night and was accepted by him as he was. According to Jesus Nicodemus, like everyone else, was in need of a conversion of heart. Remember the Samaritan woman at the well, for whom Jesus initially acknowledged no responsibility. She elicited from him his aid in the healing of her memories. Finally, Mary Magdalen, sinner *par excellence* in the world's sight, exploiter for her own security of the sinfulness of others, poured forth her loving repentance in expensive ointment and tears, to the scandal of Judas, himself a scandalously enigmatic figure[3] whom also Jesus loved.

Jesus' love for the poor and for sinners, the good shepherd's love which led him to seek always the one who was at once most open and most in need, whether on the surface of high or low degree, brought him a range of burdens which by his Father's decree he was no longer allowed consciously to carry in a life-affirming sense. What in the end and to the end he continued to carry was sin, the whole burden of mankind's guilty alienation from the true God. In the end: for the bearing of this burden was all that remained to him. To the end: for in shouldering this burden he chose to die, not under a death-wish but in obedience to the Father's unknown design. I have already argued that in considering such suffering we have no point of comparison, no frame of reference. Against this it has recently been propounded that others have suffered more and for a much longer time in concentration camps, etc. This attempt to quantify individual human suffering in Jesus' disfavour risks trivializing the Gospel; but even so crass a misunderstanding of the New Testament's claim on behalf of Jesus can help to concentrate the mind more precisely on what is distinctive in that claim. (It seems worth mentioning, despite what is said in the next paragraph, that Martin Hengel's book, *Crucifixion*,[4] makes clear that this was a peculiarly horrible form of execution. Never underestimate physical suffering.)

'Is there any sorrow like unto my sorrow?' Clearly, in terms of the above-mentioned attempt to measure suffering, the application of these words to Jesus is wholly arbitrary, being quite unwarranted by what he endured. Crucifixion, after all, was a relatively commonplace penalty, and there is nothing in the Gospels to suggest that he was treated with exceptional brutality by the standards of the age. Nor was he the first, nor yet the last man, to be unjustly condemned to death. It is not at all at these levels that the disciples glimpsed the distinctive note of Jesus' ordeal; but rather in the fact that it was this man undergoing these things. There is no protracted dwelling on the specific torments of the passion, but rather a dispassionate account, with snatches of dialogue hinting at what was really going on, namely the crisis in Jesus' relationship with the Father, with all the implications that relationship, and therefore this crisis, had for his life and mission. There is in the passion narratives the recapturing of a note of awed bewilderment in the presence of a level or quality of suffering beyond his friends' immediate grasp and yet so distinctive that nothing could ever be the same afterwards, not just for them but for their world in any of its aspects.

There is one sentence which pinpoints, perhaps more than all the rest, this absolutely distinctive note in Jesus' anguish. It is this marvellously compact and potent statement: 'He who was without sin was *made sin* for us.' Sin is alien to God, sin really does alienate human beings from God and from one another. In its most radical form it is experienced not so much as anything man does or does not do in any particular set of circumstances, but as a chronic condition of inability to relate, a state accompanied by guilt. Jesus, in taking this sin on, knows the consequent isolation and dereliction *in its pure state*, in unalloyed contrast and indeed contradiction with his earlier experience of the Father's intimate love, an experience which was his by nature. Through the resurrection of Jesus crucified the bereaved disciples came to see his true and distinctive burden as having been the burden of sin in this sense. Only when that burden was shown to them as lifted in his being raised from the dead could they retrospectively glimpse the true dimensions of his suffering. Then they could not but cry out in joy and praise of the sinless victim, the lamb who was slain not so much by the leaders and the executioners as by being made sin for us, out of love.

Current Christian attitudes to sin tend to distort it by appeal either to a reductionist form of psychology or to humanistic moralizing. Edward Norman drew attention to the latter trend in particular in his Reith Lectures.[5] Whole segments of humanity are in effect, though not of course in so many words, prematurely 'absolved', or declared not really to have sinned, on the grounds either of what their parents did to them long ago, which allegedly leaves the children without any real reason for guilt; or in the name of 'historic' injustices, which in constituting a people as oppressed render them sinless.

These reductionist attitudes ignore the hold sin exercises well beyond the reach of psychotherapy or moralism. Any exclusive appeal to these nostrums flies in the face both of experience and of the New Testament witness to how sin came to be forgiven. The wages of sin is death, the void, relationlessness; and it was so, and came by his chosen ones to be seen to be so, for Jesus: not just his act of dying but his guiltless, nameless dread. He alone effectively paid sin off by the endurance of a quality of suffering for which, as we have seen, there is no precedent or parallel in mankind's story.

The New Testament's conclusion is clear enough: only Jesus *could* take this step. The claim of his followers here is much more than the idea that it just happened to fall to his lot to be the one thus to suffer. Their retrospective conviction, based on all they knew of him and shared with him, was that it could only have been Jesus who thus obeyed to the end. It had to be Jesus who initiated a new way of obedience in and for mankind. Something in their contact with him convinced them of this at a depth beyond argument, in such a way that the notion of any other redeemer, prior, contemporary or subsequent, could find no place. In this man the comprehensive act of man's salvation had been accomplished, and it only remained for the fruits of that act in the outpouring of the Holy Spirit in people's hearts to be gathered in.[6] There was neither need nor room for another redeemer, not because they were sectarian but because they knew the crucified Jesus raised in power, as the first-fruits of the new creation. 'When I be lifted up, I shall draw all men to myself': in the disciples' minds it would have been not only betrayal but sheer, destructive folly to apply their energies and aptitudes to any task other than to become more and more effective catalysts or channels of this drawing.

12

Death-spasm

_____

The phenomenon of Jesus' life and ministry was experienced within a people whose belief was the most developed form of monotheism the world had known. The Jewish people already had a special sense of a truly personal God-with-them which was decisively intensified and rendered immediate for the disciples by Jesus himself. The prophetic tradition had begun to perceive 'God with us' as meaning more than 'God on our side against all other peoples'; Jesus definitively furthered this strand by showing forth the nearness, the intimacy of a God who was on the side of all mankind in the sense that his loving forgiveness was available in the shape of his own life, Jesus' own life, being for all.

It can therefore be said that only the Jewish tradition could have produced Jesus: the situation produced him[1] in the sense that successive and varied purgations of the Jewish spirit in creative response to oppression, disaster and exile disposed this people for his coming. There is nothing mechanistic in this conclusion – the options remained open at every stage of the redemptive process. It is merely an echo of the New Testament belief that Jesus made sense only against the background of the deepening and broadening of Jewish religious consciousness which was the fruit of the interaction between the God of Abraham, Isaac and Jacob and a remnant at least of the people in the critical events of their history.

Now the impact of Jesus himself on his followers was more than a further degree of this deepening: he was a new beginning, a new kind of God-consciousness. His work was done in exemplary fidelity to the spirit of what the Lord had done in the past, but he redefined that past as a preparation for his coming: 'Your father Abraham longed to see my day.' This truth seems forced to us only in so far as we lack a properly organic sense of our own or any other history. The past is only important because it has happened. Jesus, in redefining the past, redefined God, whom he identified with himself in relation to the Father. The God he offered was much more than a merely enlarged and more civilized version of Israel's picture of her God.

In identifying the kingdom with himself at this stage of its coming into being, Jesus had exceeded the role of prophet, priest and king in the kind of authority he had claimed and exercised. 'You would have no power over me,' said Jesus to Pilate, 'if it had not been given you from above.' Having accepted his authority his disciples could only see his death as the absence or withdrawal of God. The darkness which covered the earth during the three hours on the cross makes the point, as do the other terrifying events reported by Matthew as coinciding with Jesus' death: 'and, behold, the veil of the temple was rent in twain from the top to the bottom; and the earth did quake and the rocks rent . . .'

There is no crumb of comfort in these images. They are commonly scaled down, to become part of the common stock of signs and portents available to the purveyors of legend, as if Matthew's account had no more significance than Shakespeare's version of the preternatural happenings on the eve of Julius Caesar's murder. To me they speak of something much deeper, to be spoken of only with awe: a final convulsion not only of God-awareness but of a Godward universe, a convulsion known as the death-spasm to those with eyes to see.

Now was the world's back broken; the darkness
Heaved in half, the wells rose up in walls
And fell in floods; and earth's own gorge
Rose and retched out its coffins. Everywhere
Lightnings lashed, and the curled thunder rolled
Its bolts over the crowd that broke and ran before its crash.
Each flash showed them in a different flight.

And in the downpour only the soldiers stood
Sodden and awed beneath the Cross. 'This was the son of
   God!'
To them the eliminating moment was
The illuminating one. Now all was still.[2]

The feel of Matthew's narrative here is of *everything* being
involved in this decisive convulsion, quite definitely the end
and yet, mysteriously, the beginning. The darkness, the dead
men and the veil's rending occupy the foreground. Normal life
hardly obtrudes. As far as the disciples are concerned, the time
of Jesus' passion and death is characterized by the sudden
remoteness of God succeeding upon a time when God was
known as unprecedentedly near. Once Jesus had come to be
known, as he clearly was in the Galilaean ministry, as 'heaven's
hub',[3] his dying could only be an immeasurable hollowness. An
incomparable flow of life, energy,[4] healing and forgiving power
is suddenly and inexplicably cut off after immersing and
redirecting them. It is in this 'power cut' condition that the
risen Lord finds them.

The Gospel accounts of events between Jesus' death and the
discovery of the empty tomb offer a different but confirmatory
emphasis: after blood, sweat and tears a sense of clear,
awesome emptiness. There is a significant parallel in the
disconcerting sense of relief, of everything being without weight
or substance, of having entered a timeless and no longer
burdensome world which is so common a feature very early in
bereavement. Yet this comparison hardly matches the strange,
cool finality hinted by these accounts.

The conventional note of a dire dénouement in a tragic
history is notably absent: nothing to suggest anything like
Elizabeth I's hysterical reaction to the realization that her
signature had killed her royal cousin.[5] Such readily understandable and profound grief and guilt may have occurred,
either in the authorities or in the disciples; if so, they were of
little or no moment here compared to the deepest note, a sense
of clean hollowness, a mysteriously total clearing of the air.

The tautness of the passion accounts is succeeded by an

atmosphere of pure, purged finality. The tone of the burial stories is that of a simple ending without loose ends, an ending which is experienced as so simple and so ultimate that nothing more can conceivably happen. The intention of the women to honour the body in the tomb is in this spirit: this at least will be done, for there is absolutely nothing else to do. Drama in any recognizable sense enters only with the reaction of the leaders of the people who arrange for the tomb to be guarded. It has already been emphasized that these leaders did not play a truly central part, despite superficially holding all the trumps. They were merely continuing to act in character in a world which the important people, the 'little flock', knew as having already come to an end.

There is more to be said. In the death of Jesus Judaism was finished as the prophetic arrow-head of man's religious quest, and as the focal point of God's affair with mankind. This would hold good even if most Jews had given their allegiance to the risen Lord. The disciples knew Jesus as the rebirth and flowering of their own past, of the whole history of their people. He was the unexampled nearness of the God whom this people worshipped. 'By their fruits you shall know them': his friends had known the fruits of his intimacy with the Father, and had accepted his identification of the kingdom with himself-in-relation-to-the-Father. When he died, therefore, nothing mattered any more. (The substance of this paragraph is without prejudice to the view expounded by Ben F. Meyer in *The Aims of Jesus*[6] that the split between Christians and Jews is the most critical of all the divisions among humankind.)

And this, in a world in which only the disciples could even begin to acknowledge the real state of things, was in fact the position. If the coming of Jesus was the watershed in man's dealings with God as pinpointed in God's hitherto developing relationship with Israel, then Jesus' death in blood meant that all that remained of God and his world, despite the appearances, the normal busyness of the authorities and the people, was a shadow-land, a hopeless, timeless limbo. Given that the only people who mattered at that moment were the disciples, the elect of the Master, they alone saw the unreality of the solid world of other people and their God.

At some point the conviction that Jesus was without sin became central to the early believers' articulation of the saving meaning of these cataclysmic happenings. Sinlessness is in a way a weak word to express that quality of being fully attuned always and everywhere to the enactment of the Father's loving will. The sinless man puts no obstacle in the way of God's saving purpose either by taking short cuts or by periodic refusals to serve. This quality put Jesus in a uniquely exposed position.

Jesus, the sinless man, took the world's evil upon himself. It is fatally easy to imagine that his sinlessness lightened this colossal burden. The fact is that for this sinless man evil is quite peculiarly burdensome, because he sees it for what it is, a pervasive and relentless power threatening to overthrow all creation. He has a uniquely clear perception of the nature and scale of the conflict in which the human race is involved. Precisely because of this clarity and his consequent sureness of touch in the affairs of men, his burden is uniquely total: it is all men's burden, the whole world's burden, the burden of an unredeemed creation unequivocally recognized and requiring unprecedentedly drastic action. In all human dealings it is the person whose perception is most acute who has most to bear, as, for instance, the commanding officer who, unlike his subordinates, knows the real odds in the forthcoming battle.

Far from being a half-man, an outlandish freak, Jesus is truly man in the sense of the true man: his humanity is normative. We must resist the persistent tendency to see him as somehow less than or other than this if we are to grasp his role as saviour.

Anyone who thinks he knows adequately what it is to be human and then seeks to fit Jesus into the picture is bound either to fail utterly or to falsify Jesus; for Jesus does not fit within the confines of any of man's ways of defining himself. The history of Christian theology is littered with the noble failures and strangely contorted interpretations of those who, at least in their writings, could not get beyond their need to constrict Jesus to their own measure. The purpose of such endeavours in the modern world is to present Jesus as convincingly human,[7] but since he himself is the one authentic frame of reference for the question of what man is, the enterprise founders, because it starts at the wrong end. In its extreme form this error takes it for granted that no human being can work miracles or be raised from the dead. As Pannenberg has remarked, 'If the historian approaches his work with the conviction that "the dead do not rise", then it has already been decided that Jesus also has not risen.'[8]

The thrust of the life of Jesus creates or reveals a radical tension in human life which must be sustained and dwelt upon if we are to grow in his spirit. If we are side-tracked into a loss of concentration we are disabled from seeing the nature of the struggle and the shape of Christ's victory over evil.

What did it mean that Jesus lived surrounded by sin, by people whose sin had given evil a paralysing purchase on their lives? An effort of imagination is necessary if we are to avoid a trivial or cheapening answer which takes the extraordinary tension out of the encounter with Jesus. A creation fissured by evil in a myriad ways, a humanity enslaved to sin, could not co-exist with such a man, nor he with it. 'The children of this world are wiser in their generation than the children of light.' Someone so alive, with such a clear, direct, God-filled life, could not be tolerated. The mere presence of such a person forced the issue, making overt the contradiction at the heart of history.

If it is replied that this person was love itself, the point is strengthened. True love has a clear gaze far removed from infatuated blindness or romantic wishful thinking. Remember that it was Peter whom Jesus once called Satan: the issue was too crucial for anything mealy-mouthed. In the New Testament love and truth are inseparable companions.

In saying that Jesus, whose life was ruled by loving obedience to the Father, drew all the evil in the world upon himself, I mean much more than the sin of that generation in which he walked the earth. Their sin is the bringing out into the open of all evil in face of the threat to the reign of sin presented by the sinless man. If he was allowed to live, man's hardness of heart, the result of his complicity with evil, was threatened at its roots. He had to be eliminated. His presence had begun to bring out into the light of day all that men would have preferred to keep hidden under cover of darkness. Sinful man's cover was being blown. That he offered healing and forgiveness is not directly the point here. His whole life was an affirmation that the issue was being faced, that evil was being effectively grappled with, and that humanity was being brought to an intensely painful new birth. Too much entrenched illusion was at stake for him to be allowed to live. The devil knew his enemy, and knew exactly how to exploit humankind's instinctive, inertial fear of transformation.

So Jesus had to die, and at the hands of men, if the logic of the incarnation was to be complete and the issue resolved. It is logical that the coming of a sinless man into a world of sin results in his execution in degradation. The infancy narratives strongly suggest that it is already Jesus' destiny to engage creation's conflict at its very centre, or to become himself the centre, and in so doing to suffer the full consequences. From the Draconian measures of Herod against the rumoured child to the prophecy of Simeon to Mary: '. . . this child . . . is destined to be a sign that is rejected – and a sword will pierce your own soul too – that the secret thoughts of many may be laid bare,' this dark destiny is implied.

What makes the difference is not stoical resignation or moral dignity in the face of injustice, but loving, anguished obedience, which gives the evil in the heart of man the chance fully to enact itself at his expense. In becoming the willing victim, it is as if Jesus encourages evil to go as far as it can, to do its worst, to gather up and direct all its energies to his destruction. In the crescendo of collision between the world's sin and the sinless one Jesus refused to fight on the world's terms. This refusal forced evil to go further, to overreach itself.

So it came about that this collision, this helpless victimhood, became the turning-point. When Peter preached the risen Lord to the Jews he spoke of 'this Jesus whom you crucified' without any note of recrimination against them, for he knew now that their sin, which was of course matched by his own betrayal, had played its part in the winning of the victory, in terms of which 'all things co-operate unto good'. In killing Jesus, or in denying him, or in simply running away, these people did what any group of people would have done if faced with such a man, the innocent one, not simply a very good and courageous man.

The resurrection declares that this death was in reality the final sacrifice. In seeking to foreclose the issue of Jesus, the question raised in the person of Jesus, evil has exhausted its power. In lovingly enduring without interior rebellion his own disintegration the crucified victim has offered nothing to evil's grasp. Evil could get no hold on him and so, in encompassing his destruction, has enabled him to be raised up and shown forth as the first-born of a new humanity. The death of Jesus was the ultimate act of love, the effective offer of forgiveness for all sin everywhere at all times. This offer is not dependent on our repentance, but seeks in a free relationship of love to elicit it. First we need to allow the risen Lord, bearing his wounds, to show us in the unerring accuracy of his love our real sin.

Forgiveness is the heart of the matter, and the problem is always in ourselves, as the chapter on the wounded self suggested. The sinless, whole, wholly loving person is seen as a threat by whatever in us is as yet untouched by grace. Here again an aspect of bereavement can be illuminating: the sense of the beloved having entered a purified and exalted state in which the whole person is revealed can come as a threat to the survivor. In other words there is nothing automatic or magical in the influence of a sinless person, whether Jesus himself or another whom in death he has rendered free from sin. The offer of forgiveness, while unconditional in both cases, is not without its painful consequences in terms of facing oneself. So the temptation is to turn away from the newly-revealed sinlessness back to 'normal life'. The response is never pre-empted when God's love is in play. Remember the curious repetition of the risen Jesus' question to Peter at the lakeside: 'Do you love me?' This is Peter's opportunity to come to terms with the past in the light of the resurrection, and so to be set free for his missionary task.[9] Absolutely everything is staked on the integrity of his renewed relationship with Jesus, who as we have seen had become the focus of such intense and deeply contradictory reactions, not the least of which was guilt.

13

The Hinge of Memory

Fear and its milder brothers, dread and anticipation, first soften the tablets of memory, so that the impressions which they bring are clearly and deeply cut, and when time cools them off the impressions are fixed like the grooves of a gramophone record, and remain with you as long as your faculties. I have been surprised how accurate my memory has proved about times and places when I was frightened . . .[1]

This extract from Oliver Lyttelton's reflections on his participation in the First World War provides an incisive way in to a range of considerations on the role of memory in our lives and especially in bereavement. In this connection it may seem obvious that memory is central in the Christian experience: initially the personal memories of the disciples and the group memory of those to whom they preached. But if it is agreed that it is memory of a dead man which constitutes the body of Christian believers, it must still be asked how this can be.

To Lyttelton's assertion that fear promotes lucid and lasting memory I should want to add a similar claim for guilt. This link may seem more complex, yet when guilt finds an unequivocal centring on an event and my part in it the effect on 'the tablets of memory' is often similar to that of fear. As a boy I was shown by a bird-loving friend two baby birds which he had carefully rescued from a shattered and abandoned nest. To my distress, for at the time I had no ease with the Lord's creatures, he placed the birds in my hand. I soon managed to drop them on the concrete path on which we stood. My friend's face registered such dismay that I can still remember the moment in detail: I felt hopelessly, helplessly guilty, thirty-five years ago. This guilt was reinforced by the flat announcement the next day that the tiny birds had duly died in the night.

Later, guilt focussed on events which the world at least would call more important than an accident to two baby birds. The effect on memory was identical. After the suicide of a friend in which I was closely involved the event, along with its immediate antecedents and consequences, became so indelibly etched on my memory that the picture shows no sign of fading today, twenty-one years on. Fear and guilt were pervasive, and the outline and atmospheres of those events have a sharper edge than anything else I can recall. Indeed the outline is in some respects clearer now than before. A clutter of peripheral detail with no direct bearing on the crisis has fallen away. I can recall not only my own conflicting reactions but the reactions of others at each stage: the anticipatory anxiety of doctor and psychiatrist, the near-hysteria of some nurses and the controlled and impressive compassion of others, the embarrassment of the priest called from the altar to absolve and anoint my friend in his last agony; the suitably grave mien of the stolid policeman who, having asked the appropriate questions, sought to reassure me that I bore no responsibility. All these and others I saw then, and can see now, with a mysterious detachment, as if they were actors in a play which they did not understand; or as participants in a mystery into the unfolding of which I was being initiated, while they merely played their allotted parts. This memory remains after the fear has been lifted and the guilt dissolved, as will be explained later.

Earlier chapters have pointed out that in the preparation for and the enactment of the passion the disciples experienced a peculiarly traumatic breach in their relationship with Jesus, a breach in which fear and guilt were writ large. That is where his death left them, and there is evidence of fear and guilt in those who saw him risen from the dead. The connection between fear, guilt and memory is even perhaps strengthened when the fear concerned is that special awe or dread in face of the *mysterium tremendum* to which Rudolf Otto drew attention in *The Idea of the*

Holy.[2]

If, then, guilt and fear tend to etch clear and lasting memory, there is reason to think that it was so for the disciples in relation to the passion–resurrection sequence. This vital point in favour of accurate remembering at once raises the more interesting and less explored question of the role of memory in the disciples' lives. To put the question in a more pointed way, can we find parallels to their need to recall certain events again and again; and in particular, are there parallels to their need to centre their lives upon the memory of a death? What of their sense that it was appropriate to draw others into this centring? Centuries of custom have dulled us to the need to look for connections here, in the evoking of a death in extreme degradation not as a sadness passively remembered, not just as a desperate gesture in defiance of tragedy, but as something to be re-appropriated in praise, thanksgiving and vibrant expectation.

Pursuit of these and related questions will be crabwise, offering points of reference from other spheres to suggest that the role played by the disciples' memory of Jesus' death and resurrection can be given recognizable contours, without jeopardizing the unique content of that memory.

For instance, those psychiatrists who emphasize traumas in infancy as the root of psychic disorder in adult life aim to bring the original incident into consciousness. That on which fear and guilt focussed when things first went wrong must be brought into view. 'Going wrong' here means distorting or blanking out that moment of extreme and perhaps intolerable stress; since this repression cannot achieve more than partial success, the person's subsequent life is obscurely dominated by that early moment.

Hence, for example, Dr Janov's primal scream,[3] the heart-cry welling up from the deep self now confronted by and living through for the first time the full dimensions of that earlier and repressed anguish. That anguish was compounded of rage, fear and guilt. In that primal incident there occurred a real and lasting breach of relationship with the parent, however latent that breach might have seemed at the time. From the fact that the relationship with the parent was the infant's whole world stems the radical disablement for relationship which has persisted through childhood into the world of adulthood. To put this right, says Janov, the incident which caused the blockage must be relived in such a way as to release the repression: there must be a successful negotiation of the fence which caused the first fall. If Dr Janov's method is to succeed, the role of memory is clearly crucial. If the infantile memory continues unavailable to the patient the treatment fails.

What is at stake here is not only the importance of remembering, but the need and the capacity to reactivate and so to live more completely the moment of the breach in relationship. The conscious reclaiming of a past trauma thus becomes creative in the healing of the foundational breach and the consequent release of the energies of the self for unfettered relationship. Whether or not Janov's treatment works, there is a wide consensus within the world of psycho-analysis that some form of reliving of past traumas can be life-enhancing.

In stark contrast is Joseph Conrad's *Lord Jim*.[4] The protagonist of this novel emerges as a person hounded by a moment in his past. As a young seaman he had deserted his almost sinking ship in a moment of panic, leaving the passengers to take their chance against the elements. Thenceforward he was imprisoned by guilt, his self-image permanently shadowed by the memory of this compulsive flash of cowardice. He traversed sea and land not, like the unscrupulous Pharisee, 'to make a single convert', but to escape this implacable judgment. His betrayal of responsibility found no forgiveness, whatever compassionate encouragement he received. Useless for Jim to be told that there was nothing he could have done to save the passengers; or that he hardly knew until afterwards what he had done; or that the senior members of the crew had made his position on deck untenable by abandoning ship before him; or that no man's soul could be irretrievably lost in one aberrant moment, however grave. All these things he knew already, but the guilt went deeper, as is guilt's way, than these commonsensical observations.

Jim knew that when the time of trial had come he had failed, and was hag-ridden by the detailed memory of his failure. This he grimly determined to live down by accepting and honouring spectacularly improbable responsibilities in a new sphere in the Far East where he would not be publicly associated with the disaster. Jim behaves, then, as if he could start again without his past. In effect he treats his memory as irredeemable. His story has therefore to remain a closed book, untold and untransfigured, so that he can do nothing which is not negatively ruled by his first failure. For Jim, as for the disciples, memory of cataclysm is central, but nothing is being done with his memory. A past tragedy which is never exposed to healing possibilities cannot reveal its true meaning, and thus exerts a baneful influence on the present. This polar opposite of what happened to the disciples suggests that memory is not neutral, and cannot be merely circumvented. Something has to be done with it.

Further reflections on my memory of the incident mentioned earlier are apposite at this stage. This abiding memory might not unreasonably be thought to indicate a morbid fixation. This friend was at the time of his death the dominant influence over me, and stood at the living centre of the community in association with which the most formative years of my adult life were spent. It was inconceivable to me to treat his death, for all the horror, grief, guilt and fear which surrounded it, as something to be merely survived. That death had from the beginning a living meaning; far from being forgettable, it demanded to be shared. Yet my interpretation of the death, as of its major antecedents and consequences, has markedly changed in subsequent years. The visual and chronological picture is the same, but the tone and texture of the story have altered as a more comprehensive picture has been able to declare itself.

Light in the present has radiated powerfully into the past, showing that a death which at the time was called by some a tragedy, by some a martyrdom, by others the fruit of madness and by others again a mortal sin of pride, is within the providence of the living God. In the immediate aftermath someone sent me a note quoting these words of Jesus: 'No sparrow falls to the ground without your heavenly Father knowing it.' I swept this aside, but ten years later found in it a healing aptness.

It became clear that seemingly contradictory assessments might all have truth, each immediate interpretation being partial in both senses of that adjective. I no longer needed to struggle with these contesting partialities, which found their place in a renewed memory, the dreadful end coming through as a hope-filled instance of all things co-operating unto good, not least in the lives of those who had no understanding of this man's life and death. What disposed me for this change was the attempt to live out of my earlier and more partial memory of these events. This inadequate and botched venture ground to a halt, but the very failure of this blinkered discipleship[5] proved to be the disposition for a new horizon which cleansed my perception of the past.

This cleansing did not, of course, occur automatically. Later events were the medium of my release from the partial paralysis of the post-suicide years. I had got stuck, but I was, blessedly, stuck with a memory. To hold to this memory, or to encourage it to retain its strong purchase on mind, heart and imagination, was all I could do. My identity, my sense of my own life, was bound up with these remembered events. There was a fidelity, so that the enduring memory, at times in danger of becoming an imprisonment, became instead material for transfiguration.

The way forward came with specific ministries of forgiveness, deliverance and inner healing. The effect of these on memory was to free it from its clamp, releasing me into a newly vibrant world in which the dead person, his community and my own involvement took on a more fluid shape. This was not because the central memories were taken less seriously, but because they ceased to be the exclusive frame of reference. I was set free from the idolatrous trap of a static memory by the centring of my life for the first time on the living Lord. As I breathed this new air the remembered events attained heightened significance as a primary locus for me of the working-out of that holy mystery of God's work of salvation which encompasses all things. Particular memories ceased to be the exclusive housing of life-giving truth. That human story became caught up in and dynamically contributive to a tale without horizons other than those of hope. In other words, memories which had become boxed-in and therefore impotent became revitalized.

The parallels between this sequence and the story of the disciples may perhaps speak for themselves, although in their case the time-scale is telescoped. Their remaking had to deal with the roots of fear and guilt. In particular, there is a peculiarly intimate association between death and guilt, that radical guilt which we all know without being able to explain. In bereavement characteristic forms of what might be called symptomatic guilt are a sense of hopeless unworthiness in relation to the dead person, a sense of having somehow hastened or caused the death, and a guilty reaction to one's own resentment at being abandoned by the person who has died. We cannot think our way out of these and other negative reactions: such elements are all potentially binding, and can immobilize the proper work of remembering.

It would seem that one function of the resurrection appearances, as of the ministrations which I in time received, was to exorcize the roots of such guilt, along with fear and resentment. In other words, one job the appearances did was to free the disciples from those aspects of the past which, being binding, threatened to distort their relationship with Jesus and therefore their perception of his role as living Lord of all.[6] This strand is most evident in the story of Thomas in the Upper Room, in the haunting conversation between the risen Jesus and Peter at the lakeside, and in the account of the grumbling, dispirited pair who initially failed to recognize him on the Emmaus road.

The raising of Jesus from the dead came to be seen by the early church as the decisively effective declaration of the Father's love for humankind. At the heart of that declaration was forgiveness and reconciliation, both of interior and exterior conflict. But at the beginning, in the days immediately after the crucifixion, those who most desperately needed such reconciliation in relation to the life and death of Jesus were those closest to him, his chosen and intimate companions. Those who went on to become the first witnesses to what God was doing in this whole complex of events had first to experience for themselves, and in the present, the reconciling power of the one who had died. Clearly the appearances mediated this power and so prepared the ground for the Holy Spirit to move them into mission.

A setting in which it would make good sense for the appearances to function in this way is suggested by the witness of the bereaved. It has been most aptly said that whereas in the case of a physical wound it is wise to forget the injury once it is healed, the opposite is the case in bereavement:

> In mourning . . . the cause of the injury, the loss of an important person, *must not be forgotten*. Only when the lost person has been internalized and become part of the bereaved, a part which can be integrated with his own personality and enriches it, is the mourning process complete . . . (my emphasis).[7]

Chapter 2 suggested that bereavement itself is not the wound, but this need not contradict the stress on memory in this extract. Many workers in the field agree with Lily Pincus that the process of internalization is the most important task facing the bereaved. Early in bereavement, and the length of time involved here varies, 'the bereaved is . . . in touch with the external presence of the lost person'. This reference to the external presence and its transience is drawn from observation of a considerable range of bereaved people.

Dependence on the external presence diminishes as internalizing proceeds, but it can hardly be said too often that this has nothing to do with forgetting. Indeed it has everything to do with a purified remembering, for it is at this point that memory becomes more fully available: '. . . the bereaved becomes able to draw on memories, happy or unhappy, and to share these with others, making it possible to talk, think or feel about the dead person'. Thus anyone who negotiates bereavement without disaster finds that memory has a central place. There is every reason to suppose that the disciples shared the characteristic and positive need of the bereaved to remember, and the ability of people who have undergone critical ordeals to remember reliably.

It follows that if we take bereavement seriously as the setting for all that happened to the disciples after Jesus' death, it becomes impossible to think of them creating stories about their beloved Master, or allowing stories invented by others to make decisive headway. Any such tendency would be both unnecessary and offensive from the point of view of the bereaved. Unnecessary, because of the abundant resources of memory; offensive, because cheapening to the lovingly remembered reality. Above all, dealing in legends would work against that re-appropriation of memory without which the bereaved remain locked in the past, or in a wishful-thinking version of the past.

It is reasonable to suppose that the bereaved disciples underwent such a re-appropriation. Their confident outward movement at Pentecost would suggest that the internalizing of the 'lost' Jesus had been joyfully completed. In psychological terms, successfully to internalize a person who has died involves a clarification of memory. Put more provocatively, the most reliable memory is a transformed or redeemed memory.

If it is objected that to appeal to such a patterning is to deny the gratuitous character of what took place, I answer with the tag: 'Grace does not abolish nature but perfects it.' Moreover, to argue that the disciples went through a sequence of changes comparable to other bereavements does nothing to undermine any of the claims they came to make for Jesus. It is only to draw attention to the credibility of the supposition that reliable memories of a dead person played an overwhelmingly decisive part in everything that happened afterwards.

I 4

The Future of Memory

This was a rough death, there was nothing tidy about it,
No sweetness, nothing noble.
. . .
Still, that is how things always happen, lousily,
But later on, the heart edits them lovingly,
Abstracts the jeers and jags, imports a plan
Into the pain, and calls it history.
We always go back to gloss over some roughness,
To make the past happen properly as we want it to happen.[1]

The tendency to romanticize or tidy up the past is sufficiently
universal to suggest that it might have been operative in the
composition of our texts, especially allowing for the fact that the
process is normally half-conscious at most. Yet the remarkable
thing is how large the 'jeers and jags' loom, not least in the
shape of the inadequacies and worse of the disciples, the
recurrent anger, anguish and desperation of Jesus and the
intransigent mysteriousness of his words and deeds. While
these accounts have a definite shape or shapes, a distorting
smoothness is very little in evidence. Either the evangelists felt
no need to 'gloss over some roughness' or they were under very
powerful inner compulsion not to do so. To say that both these
elements were present is consistent with all that has been
claimed for the role of a renewed memory in bereavement.

It seems most likely that the formative factor here was the
living memory of the original group of disciples, appropriately
re-interpreted by them in the Spirit and handed on to their
early converts. The austere shape comes, I suggest, from a

progressive purification of memory not uncommon among the bereaved and more widely acknowledged elsewhere in, for instance, the interpretation of dreams. Such a possibility can only be ruled out a priori if it is assumed that the note of tragedy, disintegration and loss is the last word about being human. We should resist the assumption that any retrospective seeing of a positive shape in events is necessarily at odds with how things were – unless the shape happens to be in general Marxist or Freudian![2]

My argument does not necessitate every single detail being accurate in the sense of a collection of synchronized video-tapes, nor yet the absolute absence of any later legendary accretion. The point is that the whole thrust of my exploration of the theme of memory suggests it is wildly improbable that true memories of the central saving events of the Passion and Resurrection story became substantially distorted or embroid-ered to make a more appealing or compelling tale. If this suggestion is accepted it must be asked why so much prevalent New Testament scholarship has espoused an extreme improb-ability; but that question must await the next chapter.

In a Radio 4 discussion on current ways of understanding and teaching the Second World War, Brian Redhead implied by means of a rhetorical question that it is the pastness of an event which constitutes its unreality. This clever suggestion seems to me a desperate cop-out. It is not pastness but distortion or repression operative in the present which gen-erates unreality. Being free of the past is not forgetting the past. The past is important *because it has happened*: it is preparatory and formative, although not in any deterministic sense. 'The fathers have eaten sour grapes and their children's teeth have been set on edge' – how better to exemplify the reality of the past in the present?

A second speaker in the same programme complained that in Britain a dazzling light distorts our picture of the Second War, while a third said that watching most British films about the Second War was exactly like watching the World Cup Football Final of 1966, when England beat West Germany. Over-simplified memory hardly accounts for such distorted perspectives. Backward-looking nostalgia can obscure true memory, and the drastic decline in British prestige and morale since the war leads many to escape from a failure to find inspiration in the present into a past which never existed. The dazzling light shed by the nostalgia industry on the Dam Busters, or the Britons in Colditz, or even on Dad's Army, is not the light of memory, either healed or unhealed, although there are of course elements of recall in all these productions. The tone and texture is not from memory but from fantasy, fruit of a desire to evoke a world more comforting than our present shadowy predicament.

Mere recall is in any case not the fullness of memory. The most paradoxical and yet most pointed feature of a living remembrance is its thrust towards the future, as is beautifully exemplified by Edmund Blunden in a reflection on his continuing relationship with the First World War, in which as a very young man he was a combatant:

> 'I must go over the ground again.'
> A voice, perhaps not my own, answers within me. You will be going over the ground, it says, until that hour when agony's clawed face softens into the smilingness of a young spring day; when you, like Hamlet, your prince of peaceful war-makers, give the ghost a '*Hic et ubique?*', then we'll change our ground, and not that time in vain; when it shall be the simplest thing to take in your hands the hands of companions like E. W. T., and W. J. C., and A. G. V., in whose recaptured gentleness no sign of death's astonishment or time's separation shall be imaginable.[3]

Some literary critics have asserted the futility of the interaction between the pre-war aesthetic of men like Blunden and the nightmare of the trenches.[4] What business, it is implied, had anyone to write of this utterly meaningless horror in terms other than those of black comedy? Cop-out again, for it is precisely this attitude which Blunden's detailed memory of traumatic occurrences leads him to reject in favour of a meaning prompted by memory and yet with a mysterious purchase on the future. His 'I must go over the ground again' is similar to my own mental processes in the early post-suicide years. Others could not understand why I needed to return again and again to the topic of this man, his life, his words, his death and its sequel. Yet even at my most fixated these events had for me a strange but pressing future-shape which would not be denied, however improbable it often seemed.

Likewise with Blunden, who looked forward to 'that hour when agony's clawed face softens into the smilingness of a young spring day'. This is not the language of romanticism, but of a deep intimation of future regeneration which is clearly the fruit of some purgation of spirit. For Blunden, 'going over the ground again' was at once a compulsion and a preparation for a further stage of relationship, in which 'no sign of death's astonishment or time's separation shall be imaginable'. In the jargon of contemporary theology this conviction can only be described as eschatological.

It would be a mistake to treat as no more than an interesting and even exotic luxury the future-orientated memory evidenced by Blunden's experience and my own. 'Without the memory we are nothing – we are dead!' said the black American novelist Tony Morrisson in a recent Radio 4 interview, by way of comment on the current circumstances of black people in the USA. An organic link is implied between painful but formative events in the past, personal and corporate identity in the present, and grounds for hope. There is a convergence between this outlook and the Jewish notion of memory, which sustains recollection of critical events to the extent of re-enacting them with a sacramental and didactic purpose. The desirability and necessity of a living tradition thus comes clearly into play.

Frequent recall of the past is essential, for such recall looks to and disposes for the consummation of all things. People with a diminishing consciousness of their own story cannot live in expectation. If I have no story I cannot have a living hope. Living memory knows that its definitive shape and meaning are to be found in the future. Blunden's experience shows that this theme has a particularly pointed and poignant application to working with memories of the dead. Without such work what scope would there be for resurrection?

15

Dead Ends

A living text is always giving birth to meanings, as C. S. Lewis aptly said.[1] It follows that there is no need to assume that different approaches to the New Testament texts are contradictory of one another. Despite occasional dismissive references, those methods of interpretation characteristic of modern biblical scholarship have almost certainly formed an indispensable element in the background to my consideration of the death and resurrection of Jesus, in rather the way that Freudian psychology often forms an unacknowledged but crucial frame of reference in modern biography.

This strong sense of a debt owed still leaves room for fierce disagreement on particular and sometimes fundamental questions. New Testament research has made some progress towards distinguishing the teachings of Jesus from the proclamations of the early church. There are many attempts at a historical reconstruction of Jesus' life and teaching on the one hand, and of the early Christian community on the other. Yet the contributions of the scholars in the area covered by my exploration have been strangely thin. They have in general very little to say about the human dynamics of the transformation of that small group of striken disciples, with their memories of Jesus and his teaching, into the nucleus of the much larger and very different grouping which we call the early church. Much is said about the contrast between the two, little about how the change happened.

Chief among readable exponents of one fashionable analysis is Hubert Richards. The great merit of his book, *The First Easter: What Really Happened?*,[2] is that in the cause of popularization Richards expresses clearly and with éclat an outlook not uncommon in New Testament studies but rarely propounded unequivocally. Nothing happened at the first Easter apart from that transformation of the disciples which enabled them to see and act upon the true significance of Jesus. They then made a policy decision to express their faith in stories likely to commend this belief to their contemporaries.[3] In other words, the narratives of appearances and of the finding of the tomb empty did not happen as told, but the disciples judged that the first-century listener or reader would be helped by supposing that they did. Richards does not mean that any story would have served this purpose, but that certain kinds of story would have been appropriate to initiate people of that culture into the truth of Christ. This was the way insight and vision were communicated in those days.

In common with those scholars whose findings he distils Richards separates the disciples' inner change from those events which, according to the Gospels and Paul, initiated that change. This dislocation rests in part on a predisposition to think that such events cannot happen and therefore did not happen. That which the New Testament tells us convinced the chosen ones cannot have been what in fact convinced them, because such happenings are inconceivable, although acceptable enough to first-century Jews.

It is noteworthy that in *On being a Christian* Hans Küng[4] reacts similarly to the story of the Gadarene swine, mentioning almost in passing that it is almost impossible to believe that Jesus worked such a miracle. Describing the story as 'grotesque', Küng sees no need to put forward any substantial justification for this cavalier approach. The local people who witnessed the incident could not, according to the story, thus lightly shrug off the matter. Devastated by the searing power brought into play by Jesus, 'they begged him to leave their district'. The tone of the story, and particularly of this last phrase, hardly suggests that nothing happened of the kind described. Küng assumes that civilized modern man knows better than to believe such stuff of the Lord Jesus. In reality he and the local witnesses are in the same boat in finding this aspect of Jesus beyond them. It is only their methods of escape from the tension which differ. Küng seeks to rationalize it out of existence; they seek to be rid of Jesus. To say, 'this cannot have happened because it is offensive to the assumptions my culture makes about God and man' is not significantly different from saying 'Please go away. You are too alive, too real for us to cope with at the moment.'

There is also a suggestion behind work of this kind that to accept the substance of the accounts as factual is to detract from true faith, to substitute legend for what is worthy of belief. In other words, had Jesus appeared to his followers in the ways described, and had the tomb really been found empty, God would have been letting the side down by short-circuiting the need for faith. Here a predisposition obtrudes to the point of radically distorting the evidence. If the history of the people of Israel is the story of God's affair with mankind coming to crisis in the passion of Jesus, which nobody denies to have been a historical event, this crisis cannot be resolved by a sudden switch of focus, unsupported by the texts, to the coming into existence in the disciples of a new attitude to life. The predisposition involved here is oddly anti-incarnational: God's passionately total involvement with his creation of love is denied at the very point of definitive revelation, the coming of Jesus from the grave to his own, the supreme 'moment in and out of time'.

My emphasis throughout, like Richards', has been on a change or sequence of changes in the disciples. Had they not been changed the resurrection could not have been recognized as the focal point: the empty tomb and the appearances are not a bludgeon to batter the sceptic or doubter into belief. But those changes, if severed from the preceding story which supplies their context, become incomprehensible. That the disciples' Easter faith should have been born *out of nothing* would be a wonder at least as difficult to believe as any of those actually recorded in the Gospels, as Karl Barth perceived.

The nature of the disciples' involvement with Jesus, of his commitment to them and their allegiance to him, scandalized as they were by his passion and death, meant that only the emptiness of the tomb and his coming to them newly alive from the dead could give their lives and the world they knew any meaning other than having had an interesting past. They were only able to move on, only able to interpret the scriptures in his sense when they had seen him and spoken with him after his death. In the Emmaus story the risen Jesus is the interpreter of Israel's past as pointing inexorably to himself in his risen being. The texts attest that it was only in his coming to them, whatever their previous intimations and intuitions may have been, that the disciples were able to grasp this fundamental coherence and dynamism of the scriptures, as of their own allegiance to him.

This means that to deny the resurrection stories is to place a question-mark where the texts supply an explanation. The Easter narratives may be rejected, but the puzzle that they leave us with is not to be so lightly set aside.

Removal of the episodes of the empty tomb and the appearances threatens the texts as we have them with incoherence. It must be added that to maintain that these episodes are indispensable is by no means to undermine the role of faith which, as Jesus makes clear at the supper, is crucial throughout this disruptive and remaking sequence of events. It remained and remains open to the sceptic to press the counter-argument that the empty tomb could be explained otherwise and the disciples were simply deceived in thinking they had seen the risen Lord. After all, it is flatly said of the appearance to 'more than five hundred of the brethren at once' that 'some doubted'; while the pages of Papias provide striking witness to the vehemence and sophistication of anti-resurrection apologetic in the early centuries. This belief was scandalous from the beginning.

An additional consequence of excising these elements would be to alter the meaning of what is left. Resurrection minus the empty tomb and the appearances is not resurrection as the New Testament understands it. The crucified Jesus would thus have disappeared without trace and for ever from recorded history when his body was placed in the tomb, except for whatever role he might be thought to have played in dreams and visions. The manifestations of resurrection as our sources give them are at once more earthy and more convincingly heavenly than such a picture.

There is in the resurrection narratives a strong sense of a new power being shown forth in the invading by one another of worlds hitherto seen as disparate, in their coalescence, in a mysterious but irreversible mutation of humanity revealed to the wondering gaze, hearing and touch of the chosen ones.[5] There is also a simplicity, a freshness, almost an artlessness here: a lack of self-consciousness, because the witnesses become wholly caught up in the wonder of him who is seen, heard and touched. It is therefore essential to keep moving from the work of the scholars back to the text, for even the most lively scholarship cannot match these pristine characteristics which leap from the pages of the New Testament. It is as if these stories carry something of the power of the events they recount, in an almost secret form which beyond a certain point eludes analysis.

To take this ancient witness fully seriously involves acknowledging that the role of the appearances was both vital *and transitory*. Without them there would have been no setting in the disciples' lives for the release of the Spirit, no intelligible content of revelation for the Spirit to clarify and propagate. In line with the previous chapter's emphasis on the role of memory in bereavement, the sustaining of any close relationship needs some minimum of continuity, especially when it has been threatened by a traumatic break. This resumption of continuity is an important aspect of what the appearances give to the disciples as they assimilate the overwhelming implications of what has happened to them through him; but a time came when there was no longer any place for that kind of appearance. If they were truly to live henceforward in him and he in them they must not become set in a clinging, passive dependence, although visions and 'revelations' could and sometimes did abound thereafter.

What then of us, who have not seen the Lord in the way in which the disciples did? That they had a special kind of contact with the risen Lord cannot diminish whatever happens to us, but rather helps to render intelligible in faith the most improbable events in our lives. This is not to say that their witness as such gives us the answers on a plate, any more than the appearances as such gave them all the answers. The answer for us, as for them, is Jesus, in whatever way he shows himself to us as Saviour. His ways are as different as we are from one another, and as the various stages of our lives differ from each other; we who have not been bereaved of him as his disciples were do not encounter his risen being in the way in which they briefly did. In the coming of the Spirit creation moved on from that point, and in the light of that movement it is meaningless to make would-be qualitative comparisons between different ways of knowing the Lord.

In contrast with Hubert Richards, many scholars would readily accept that the Gospel narratives are the precipitate of some kind of psychic experience on the part of the first disciples. In *Jesus and the Spirit* James D. G. Dunn[6] asks 'What were the spiritual experiences which brought the infant church to birth?' – a seemingly sensible and appropriately pointed question. But if, as Dunn's form of the question impels us to do, we concentrate on 'experiences', considered as isolated incidents within the lives of the disciples, the origins of the church will appear to be located in a series of nebulous psychic phenomena.

Such a picture seems to interpret the change in the disciples by analogy with the classical conversion experience of an evangelical Christian. This is anachronistic, for the significance and power of psychic phenomena are always crucially dependent on the context within which they occur. They are not simply isolated happenings, nor are we passive recipients of them. Hence the appropriateness of seeking to locate the resurrection appearances in the setting of bereavement, seen as something which people both undergo and go through. We are asking what brought about the transformation of the followers of a recently dead man into a celebratory community, confident heralds of the risen Lord. Any answer merely in terms of certain psychic phenomena, which somehow pushed their recipients into a new stance towards life, is just as unsatisfactory as a reply which allows them to drop out altogether.

Something is needed at the nexus where bereavement issues in

Easter faith, but 'psychic phenomena' will not do the job. Notice how Dunn, in seeking to make such phenomena fulfil a role which cannot be theirs, is led into serious distortion of the textual evidence. 'The three most primitive characteristics of the resurrection appearances prior to Paul,' he writes, 'are a visionary seeing, an element of doubt and fear, and a sense of obligation to make the vision known.'[7] The phrase 'a visionary seeing' begs the question which is being asked, while 'a sense of obligation'[8] is precisely not evidenced by these narratives. We nowhere read of the disciples being driven by an inner compulsion, like the Ancient Mariner, to tell their tale to some captive and unwilling audience.

In this way Dunn's frame of reference reveals itself as just as unsatisfactory as the narrowly rationalistic apologetic on which I was reared, which treated all objections to the historical truth of the resurrection stories as the fruit of an irrational scepticism. It seemed to me bewildering that this apologetic, cogent enough on its own terms, never broached the key question: supposing that Jesus showed himself alive after his death by many proofs as recounted in the Gospels and Acts, what intelligibility and power did these manifestations have? How could they, if understood only as isolated and therefore arbitrary wonders, have had the transforming effects they undoubtedly did have? If the appearances are isolated from any identifiable human setting, whether in this way or in Dunn's, they can only provoke my boyhood response, still vividly remembered: 'So what?' Perhaps the Hubert Richards strand of thinking has glimpsed this, only to be decoyed by this negative insight into a different cul-de-sac!

Part Four

16

What Difference
Does It Make?

The Gospel calls us beyond the safe frontiers of day-to-day survival, morally respectable or otherwise, into a new kind of life which sees everything with fresh eyes full of wonder and gratitude. This is why bereavement is a suitable moment to take if we are looking for situations which might offer a hint of how it was for Jesus' friends, and how it could be for us if we were awake.

> Every moment is a beginning;
> Every moment is an end;
> And moments of crisis are sacramental of the whole:
> The eternal generation of creation
> Realized in this world of becoming.[1]

Every human crisis is potentially a growing-point precisely because it reveals the hopeless inadequacy of our thinking and behaviour-patterns just when we would most like to be able to think clearly and act decisively. Constantly, and very much against the grain of our habitual assumptions, we are being overtaken by events, like the two disciples on the Emmaus road or, in prospect, those who delay for their own reasons when the end comes. But crisis makes this predicament overt as it becomes apparent, whether in marital discord or in conflict between groups or nations, that events have a momentum of their own which we may have helped to precipitate but which now puts us at risk. We are pressed by superficially accidental circumstance to seek a new inclusive frame of reference for our life and thought. What is in fact happening in all crises, individual or corporate, is that we are being called into fuller, more authentic being. It is to this de-categorized condition, to this lostness, that the Gospel speaks with most incisive power, commending not a new philosophy but a new way of being which draws together the disparate threads of man's story and of our individual lives into a shared present transcendence of 'this bank and shoal of time'.

It is necessary to let different areas of perception and reflection collide, interact and invade one another in our hearts and minds if the Gospel is to 'come alive' for us. Remember Stephen Verney's remark, quoted earlier, about things in time and things outside time striving to express themselves in the same event. These words seem to catch the spirit of the Gospel as a whole, not just of the resurrection narratives which Verney was considering. His words also touch on a recurring quality of awakened human consciousness. But the disciples' experience of the risen Lord provides the supreme example of that translucent dimension of being and becoming to which Verney points. To this extent it is not possible to say in normally flat or round terms what happened in those Easter encounters, precisely because too much happened for that; but what happened was definitive for his friends' prior and subsequent relationship with him, as for their total perception of what is, and therefore for the good news they have handed on to us.

There is thenceforth in the disciples a passion, a compelling desire, a constraining by the Holy Spirit for the work of salvation: for the Lord is risen, which means that the last age has not only begun but presses in and through them towards completion. It should not perhaps dismay us too deeply that after this wondrous turning-point Christians down the ages have not infrequently lapsed into the preaching and practice in the name of Jesus of unimaginative and heartless dogmatism, flaccid moralism and comfortable rationalistic uncertainty. The bow-string cannot be kept taut for very long at a time, so the recurrence of these unredeemed ways in the slack of history, or of ourselves or others, need not be entirely surprising.

Such recurrences do not mean that the resurrection has made and makes no great difference. What has happened is that the life, death and rising of Jesus have so penetrated this world as to undermine the now illusory equilibrium of sin's deadly reign, forcing the issue with evil on such a scale and with such power that the tension in creation is intensified. We are told that the gates of hell will not hold out against Christ's church. If, as this image suggests, the risen life of Christ in his members reduces evil to a defensive position, there is every reason to expect total combat, for the devil now knows his enemy and is not yet disarmed. That final outcome of the spiritual warfare of which Paul speaks from experience is yet to come, when everything in us that has any complicity with the devil's way will be cast out. Until then he has a perverted power, if given half a chance, reactively to distract from single-minded concentration on the one thing necessary. It is to be expected that the furthering of Christ's victory should involve acute pain for all concerned, as the last stage of creation's travail is undergone. A pitch of tension[2] is reached when most of us most of the time seem to find it unbearable to open ourselves for long to that glimpse and assurance of glory which is the risen Lord, for to hold to him, to stay with the painful ambivalence which cannot yet be completely transcended, would cost, we know in our bones, no less than everything: 'He that shall lose his life shall save it.'

It is not easy, it is distinctly vertiginous except for the very mature, to live for long at a time with any keen sense that the barriers of space and time have already been breached and are wearing very thin. Crises offer the opportunity to be launched into a more transparent condition in which, if we can directly bear and live through the pain of the loss of earlier moorings and the uncertainty of the future, we can be made more receptive and responsive. Paul's hymn (I Cor. 13) to the 'still more excellent way' of love is an unforgettable description of this new way of strength through vulnerability, when the Holy Spirit, seeking to form Christ in us, breaks through the blockages of inherited sinfulness and consequent self-made obstructions to our coming into true being: 'Love bears all things, believes all things, hopes all things, endures all things.'[3] This love is a gift which, if it has once even touched us, is known as so natural to men that it is quite beyond any self-securing grasp; for man's real nature is to be loved by God, to receive and give with joyful spontaneity that love which is poured out in his heart by him whom man by nature seeks.

The passage into this love is a narrow way and a lonely pilgrimage, for as love makes headway, whatever evil remains in us must seek stridently or furtively to overmaster it. This we have glimpsed in the inner journey of the first friends of Jesus along the way to his resurrection, a journey coming to crisis in the ambivalence to them of his passion and death. In their sifting by Satan, we see this ambivalence in its cruelly tragic depths. As he, the sinless one, goes on his tortured way into the Father's hands it is as if the immediate consequence of his self-offering for mankind's sin was to put his chosen ones more deeply at risk at evil's hands than ever before. If he was on course, albeit in unspeakable mental and physical anguish, they were nowhere. It is not easy to find words for the quality of this desolating exposure, but the austere poignancy of the passion narratives pointedly suggest it.

Their master's course of suffering and death left them prey to a lowering darkness of unprecedented intensity. Yet this is not the grey horror of anonymous lack of meaning and purpose beloved of so many existentialists and glorified by Sartre. It is instead a specific and radical deprivation of the light they have known and in which they have lived during their three years' companionship. Yet this deprivation, while undoubtedly an emptiness, was not just a blank: Jesus, whom they knew to have had 'the words of eternal life', who had been to them the vessel of God's life enlivening them, was dead. Scandalized, sifted and emptied as they were, they did not merely forget: their faith was protected against that spirit of ultimate despair which is the outright rejection of God. They were broken open by their whole contact with Jesus, culminating in their critical ordeal. They were entering, perhaps kicking and screaming, perhaps numbed by shock and grief or shredded by anxiety, on the narrow way which leads to life.

They tell us that Jesus came to them from the dead. In thus coming he broke into and out of all the categories or frames of reference in which human beings sought, and still seek by a myriad means of their own or the devil's devising, to circumscribe and control the world of their experience. He came to them as a new world, a world in which all that had so far been partial and fragmentary came wonderfully together in the revelation of God's love winning the victory over death, the ineluctable fragmenter. There is thus in the Easter narratives an incomparable innocence, a quietly strong breathing of a newly purposeful integration. This succeeds on the cataclysmic encounter with evil newly entered on and endured by the passionate Christ in fulfilment of his destiny, his baptism.

Yet all this is a story told by faith in faithful love. While clearly not the fruit of that immature 'innocence of not knowing' which characterizes some religious people and provides ammunition for the sceptic, the gospel story cannot and would not compel assent: it is not that kind of story. This account of the definitive breaking of the sin-laden and death-dealing barriers within creation, and between creation and God, remains beyond the reach of even the ablest human wit. For the love which powered these events is the same love which makes all things, a gift by its very nature and so no respecter of persons. It is an uncovenanted outpouring for man's delight in God: 'Eye hath not seen, nor ear heard, neither hath it entered into the heart of men, what things God has prepared for them that love him.' The New Testament is full of direct and indirect evidence of the drawing of the disciples and their converts into the joyful experience of these things. The witness of the saints in every age likewise testifies that what happend in the beginning was not a flash in the pan but the initiation of the progressive transfiguration of all things, a process veiled and impeded by our blindness, deafness and hardness of heart.

Bereavement is often a place of privileged access to 'this great mystery which we worship', for in the dissolution, the letting-go of worldly securities which it hastens, there is new space in the

bereaved person's life for the Lord's coming. This is perhaps
the moment to reinforce a distinction and a connection which
are absolutely central to this book. All the New Testament
writers, says Moule, keep Jesus,

> in a category other than that to which the believer hoped to
> belong at the end. Jesus . . . is uniquely one with the Father
> and close to him, and he is the origin and active initiator of all
> that the believer may hope – derivatively and by dependence
> on him – to become. The distinction between the divine,
> creative initiative and human response and dependence and
> creatureliness seems to be clear. And as soon as Christians
> begin to think of contact with a departed friend (and Paul is,
> perhaps, beginning to do so), it is not quite in the same way
> as they think of their contact with Christ. Rather, *it is precisely
> because of him and by virtue of his divine initiative* that they find
> themselves conceiving of communion with the dead in
> Christ.[4]

It is useful to have so clear a statement of the difference
between the disciples' later relationship with Jesus and all
other bereavement experiences. This difference, of course,
consists in who the disciples perceived Jesus to be. The great
and varied range of titles and descriptions used of Jesus in the
New Testament shows the first Christians straining all available language to do any sort of justice to this person whom they
evidently saw from Whitsun at the latest as a quite new
phenomenon: the new man who, judged by what he does, can
only be divine.[5] It is even more useful for my immediate
purpose to have outlined, in the words of Moule which I have
italicized, the organic link between the resurrection of Jesus
and the communion of saints, which can come into existence
only as an extension of the resurrection.

After his encounter on the Damascus road, 'Paul knew
beyond doubt that though Jesus was no longer alive in the flesh
He was . . . so alive that Paul could never be the same again.'
Paul 'kept trying to say that even though Jesus had died and
been buried, He was more alive than He had been in the flesh.
He was really risen from the dead to take command of human

lives even more powerfully than when He had walked the earth as a man among men.' Finally, 'just as Jesus became a greater force in His risen presence, those who knew Him and loved Him walk among us in their risen presence with magnified power and influence.'[6] The blurb of Arthur Mielke's book on his own bereavement from which these remarks are taken describes him as an ordained Presbyterian minister. It is a great joy to see belief in the traditional doctrine of the communion of saints re-emerging in the Protestant churches[7] by way of reflection on personal bereavement.

The fact that a bereaved Christian can receive and be released by a variety of intimations of the resurrection of his human beloved is brought about by the raising of Jesus and is a further specification of that original fact, without which no such growth in the Spirit would be available. It is as being aggregated to Christ that the deceased person is experienced as newly alive and in a redeemed communion which has an aspect of sharing with the survivor in this world. In other words, without faith in Christ, however 'unconscious', or a first conversion in the course of the bereavement itself, this sphere cannot open up, because the bereaved's hatches are down as he struggles to survive his grief, so that the Holy Spirit cannot lovingly exploit his vulnerability. In the believer bereavement can become indivisibly a deepening of his life in Christ, a forgiven and forgiving awareness of the positive reality of the beloved in the present, and a major re-channelling of energies into new relationships and works of loving service. In other words bereavement can facilitate or prove the occasion of a big step into that joyous freedom from the law of sin which the Spirit gives. If we are never lost how can we be found? How can we give the Lord the opportunity he seeks to find us?

Consideration of the events with which the New Testament is concerned might suggest that the major focus is on a sequence of events in time, a linear sequence. But the place these events have in the New Testament as a whole suggests a sense of a mystery being worked out in time and yet not bounded by time. These things are seen as at once intensely particular, happening in a definite place at a definite time, and yet universal not merely in their moral implications but in the difference they make to all that is real. The key events of Jesus' life, death and resurrection are regarded as affecting indivisibly all relationships within creation and the relationship between creation and God. From its beginning the story of Jesus carries at every point this strange awareness of two kinds of reality meeting each other: the timeless and that which is in time. This meeting can be seen either as timeless reality breaking into time ('The Word was made flesh') or as timebound reality being opened up from within to reveal that which is beyond time (the transfiguration). In the latter case events in time declare their eternal meaning: but the resource which enables them to do so is not in time: 'The Spirit blows where it will.'

If we trust exclusively to our imagination here we shall take our imaginings too literally: we are then in danger of splitting up reality, thus missing the meaning of the dimension of becoming as reconciliation. 'God wanted . . . all things to be reconciled through him and for him, everything in heaven and everything in earth, when he made peace by his death on the cross.' An undivided reality is coming into being through and in these events, for the reign of sin which allows us to see and enact only division is overcome. That which happens in time is an expression of that which is outside or beyond time; it is also a becoming timeless. It by no means follows that only the timeless is real: to imagine this is to conjure up a world of pure mind and spirit which is not ours, while denying the value of this material creation's striving towards its goal.

Equally, reality must not be defined as essentially time-bound, for this is to deny our experience of the timeless, as Macbeth did:

Tomorrow, and tomorrow, and tomorrow,
Creeps in this petty pace from day to day,
To the last syllable of recorded time;
And all our yesterdays have lighted fools
The way to dusty death.

This feeling of time as just one damn thing after another ending in nothing is a conviction of time unredeemed: these words are spoken by Macbeth at the moment when he is told of his wife's death.

The tension between these polarities, time and the timeless, must be sustained, not evaded by the attempt to deny one or the other. Macbeth's attitude is perfectly logical, as was Peter's on the Mountain of Transfiguration when he sought to perpetuate a particular moment in a static form: 'Lord, let us make three tents . . .' Both aspects, then – the historical event in time and its timeless aspect – must be retained if a total picture is to emerge which transcends the limits of our imagination and thus puts us in touch with the universal mystery being worked out in this present sacramental moment. The New Testament understands the resurrection as meaning that Christ is powerful now to save. The wordly-wise Screwtape understood this all too well when he advised the trainee devil to do everything he could to ensure that human beings were preoccupied with the past or the future.[8] Success in this enterprise, he argued, would guarantee victory. Against this devilish wisdom at least one New Testament author holds that the fidelity of believers to Jesus and his way actually hastens the coming of 'new heavens and a new earth in which righteousness dwells'. The writer of the Second Letter of Peter tells his readers that they ought to be 'waiting for and *hastening* the coming of the day of God'. We stand in need of this exhilarating note of peacefully urgent and active expectation.

17

Predisposition
and Revelation

Anselm long ago spoke of faith seeking understanding, but it is equally valid to speak of faith enabling or releasing understanding. Yet there is a tendency to say that a person's interpretation of particular elements in the Bible depends decisively on the assumptions he or she brings to the task. While it is true that our prior assumptions can constrict our understanding, this is to my mind a mere cautionary tale masquerading as an absolute. This chapter offers a range of evidence contradicting such fatalism, including an account of how this book reached its conclusions.

It is not unknown for an object of study to break upon the student in a new way such that the elements in the existing picture fall apart and re-assemble in an unfamiliar, surprising and yet compelling fashion. The simplicity and comprehensiveness of the new pattern causes a gasp of wonderment, not least that this 'discovery' had not been noticed long ago. The distinguished scientist Sir Laurence Bragg, interviewed on television, said with disarming candour and almost boyish enthusiasm that his new insight felt from within much more like a revelation than a discovery. As far as Bragg was concerned his insight was given to him, although that gift was not unconnected with his own and his colleagues' work.

In Bragg's remarks there is a note of humble reverence, a sense of having played a crucial but given part in a process of revelation. It is a cliché that we live in a scientific age, that science has replaced religion as the prevailing frame of reference. In popular scientism a mechanistic model prevails heavily over any sense of mystery. Yet this is by no means the state of play among serious scientists. In the new frame of reference the old seems not so much wrong as unreal, or at least as having never had as much reality as was thought at the time. Nobody has satisfactorily explained the leap from the old to the new, the Archimedes moment with which Bernard Lonergan introduces his mammoth study of *Insight*.[1] But that it happens, and is central to man's understanding of himself and his world, is beyond contradiction, unless we want to turn Ecclesiastes' view that there is nothing new under the sun into the directive note of our lives. Again, the faith-question.

Teilhard de Chardin's *The Phenomenon of Man*[2] proposed a Christ-centred view of the developing cosmos, for the elaboration of which he was constrained to invent a new language. Regardless of how successful or otherwise this attempted synthesis was, the howls of rage and scorn emitted by some theologians and scientists[3] desperate to maintain the distinctiveness of their respective disciplines show that the venture touched a nerve. Teilhard was trying to take each group further than they were prepared to go, putting before them the faith-question as he saw it arising from within each sphere of thought. He was at once indicating to the theologian what a properly scientific perspective has to offer him; and to the scientist how theology might expand his horizons. Teilhard wrote the following in 1920, although it was not published until 1959 in French and 1964 in English:

> Without the process of biological evolution, which produced the human brain, there would be no sanctified souls; and similarly, without the evolution of collective thought, through which alone the plentitude of human consciousness can be attained on earth, how can there be a consummated Christ? In other words, without the constant striving of every human cell to unite with all the others, would the Parousia be physically possible? I doubt it.[4]

Seen by many not as an integrator but as an over-optimistic pantheist, Teilhard was in fact striving to put into words what he had seen, or what had been revealed to him through an intense and many-sided experience of created existence. It is noteworthy that the passage quoted was written only two years after the 1918 armistice. It was what happened to him that summoned him beyond the limits of either science or theology as then established.

Teilhard's friends begged him to record his thoughts in a properly metaphysical framework, but new wine cannot be put into old wine-skins: apart from the impossibility of the task such an attempt would have involved a degree of falsification. There is no short-cut, no way of presenting the fruits of a change of heart which will convince those who are not yet open to such a change.

A sixteen-year old schoolboy expostulated with an inspired religious teacher: 'What can I do? You have smashed my childhood ideas of religion. You have shown me that those ideas were wrong.' 'Not wrong, just inadequate,' replied the teacher. After a pause the boy said: 'My childhood ideas of religion were not really there.' This moment of truth, along with the more extended examples given in this chapter, undermine the view that in any field of human endeavour we are prisoners of the assumptions with which we begin. Newman said: 'To live is to change, and to be perfect is to have changed often,' and St John positively affirmed: 'We do not know what we shall become.'

My journey of heart and mind has taken me from the starting-point of a narrowly rationalistic apologetic of the resurrection through some misty modernistic re-interpretation to the perspective from which I now write. This book began with a long-standing hunch that there were parallels to be drawn between bereavement experiences on the one hand and the New Testament witness to Jesus' life, death and resurrection on the other. Once the pursuit of this intuition was seriously launched the parallels began to declare themselves more clearly, more deeply, and over a wider range of consciousness than I had expected. This was heady stuff, and threatened to distort perspective by fixating me on the similarities to the exclusion of possible differences and contrasts. I was in danger of the sort of limitation which characterizes Harry Williams' *True Resurrection*.[5] Williams sees resurrection everywhere, in all significant human development – e.g. in the skilled tennis player who has to die to his identification with that particular skill if he is to become more of a person.

This is in a way unexceptionable, in that if Jesus' being raised from the dead is the initiation of the transformation of the cosmos, then all development, however mundane, is part of and powered by his resurrection. Yet Williams' treatment has a blandness, a degree of psychological naivety.

He sees resurrection as happening all over the place. The snag is that the link between this many-layered process, which he describes sensitively up to a point, and the Holy Spirit's power is not central to the thesis. The relationship to Jesus which the New Testament claims as essential to salvation is at best underplayed, so that the sophistication of Williams' description of states of heart and mind is not matched by any decisive theology of the Holy Spirit. Whence comes Williams' resurrection, and where is it going? The experiences he describes are formative, but are they radically transforming? Do they initiate into the mystery of Christ, and if so how? There is a sense in which Williams is not writing about resurrection at all, at least in the gospel's terms. The admittedly remarkable resilience of the human psyche will not itself save us and raise us. What part is played by the living Lord, in allegiance to whom we must, according to Paul, 'work out our salvation with fear and trembling'?

The danger at this point in my investigation was a comparable naivety about bereavement. Excited by those of my witnesses to bereavement who saw it as enriching, I tended to conclude that just as bereavement happens everywhere, so does some form of resurrection-experience. The point about the disciples' bereavement was that it was as it were bigger and better than anyone else's, and so could and should serve as a kind of model to which other bereavements would approximate. I obscurely sensed that there was a lack of power in this analysis, not least in any effective pastoral application in the lives of people struggling with bereavement. To say to such people: 'It's all right because the disciples went through something much worse' would hardly console any but the least thoughtful. An interested enquirer asked me at this time: 'What difference does your view of bereavement make?'

I was rescued from the muddle implied by this blunt question by re-exploring the New Testament, particularly the resurrection narratives, allowing the evidence I had to hand about contemporary bereavement to interact with the texts. The more this interchange was allowed to happen, the more urgently the differences between my two data-banks pressed themselves upon my attention. A re-orientation of the work was evidently required. In other words, as the range of similarities became clearer there was less and less need or desire to minimize the differences. It was in the continuous dialogue between on the one hand my own and others' bereavement experiences and on the other my reading of the New Testament that I became convinced that there was present to the disciples' consciousness a dimension decisively different, different in kind if you will, from any other bereavement experience known to me.

This dimension can be telegraphically summarized in the New Testament's conviction that Jesus was the Saviour of the world. I became freshly aware of this staggering assertion as emerging from recapitulation of the successive stages of their relationship with him in his life, his passion and his resurrection. My question became: who was this man in relationship to whom these people felt constrained very soon after his death to proclaim him to the world in such exalted terms? Who was this man about whom it was conceivable to his followers to make such statements and sustain them against every imaginable challenge? A further range of questions was in a way prior to these: what were the successive interactions between Jesus and the disciples which had such consequences? What changes of heart, and resultant shifts in the furniture of their minds, were implied by their witness?

The quiet insistence with which these questions hit me, and the difference they made to my approach to the resurrection, to bereavement and to the mysterious truth of our salvation through Jesus' death, is almost impossible to describe. The superficially familiar texts of the resurrection narratives, sloughing off their seeming quaintness, radiated a kind of life quite new to me, while the urge to play down anything which did not square with my conventional modernism fell away. Indeed it was these hitherto awkward bits which now most awed and delighted me, suggesting in the meetings with the risen Jesus a quite fresh intimacy and power in God's relationship with man, a new way of being as yet fully entered into only by Jesus himself but in the making for us all. I met here something overwhelming rather than bizarre or para-normal. Everything in the stories came to seem appropriate, pointed, even natural, once the fact of whom the disciples were meeting had been assimilated. This was how it had been for these men and women. There was a kind of reverent matter-of-factness about it all. These and like happenings had launched the Christian proclamation. How could it have been otherwise? How could I ever have thought otherwise in the face of these enspirited narratives? God's ways are not ours. Nor, mercifully, is his time: nothing is wasted.

With what was I engaging through the eyes and ears of those huddles of early believers? Words are hopelessly inadequate, but it was a question of who rather than what; it had to do with Jesus as they then knew him and as he came to be known, in consequence of their faithful response, in any subsequent generation. For me it was – if you will – a revelation of the crucified Jesus as the living Lord who showed himself alive to his own after his passion. This was someone who is able to give, and does not hesitate to give, meaning and purpose to all suffering and death prior and subsequent to his own. This was someone for whom impossibility in any of our senses meant and means an opportunity for ever-new works of love.

This, therefore, was someone absolutely unique, someone who could only be epitomized, however unsatisfactorily, as by nature God and man. There is, it seems to me, such a thing as 'conversion by the text'! I am not arguing that we can know exhaustively or even adequately what is meant by calling Jesus God and man. Of course we cannot, but so to call him is the least we can do.

Another and complementary way of stating the difference between the disciples' bereavement and all others is in terms of the release of the Spirit. This is the only death which has come to be experienced as having the power of universal mediation, a power claimed and enacted in missionary terms by the early church. The outcome of Jesus' death according to our witnesses was the definitive release of the Holy Spirit in this world. They came in the Spirit to know his death as being the salvation of all, the forgiveness of all, the transformation of all things. The New Testament unequivocally asserts that it is only Jesus' death which renders the Spirit available. That other bereavements can focus the life of the Spirit for those involved is not denied, but without Jesus' death there would be as far as we are concerned no Spirit to focus, no divine life ready to be shared.

As we have seen, other bereaved people sometimes experience a heightened and intensified presence and influence within their immediate circle of the person who has died. Yet the releasing and making available to all and for all of a completely new form of life is never claimed, at least in any sustained or effective way, for that person's death. No death other than that of Jesus has been thus claimed as creating and offering a decisive opportunity for everybody to be lovingly shaped into our true being as vessels of praise and glory. Other deaths and other bereavements can share in this transforming power, but cannot originate it or further it of themselves. 'There is no other name under heaven by which men may be saved . . .'

18

Real Presence

The First Letter of Peter says: 'You did not see him, yet you love him; and still without seeing him, you are already filled with a joy so glorious that it cannot be described, because you believe.' This astonishingly vibrant belief on the part of those who had never seen Jesus arose from the belief of those who, having been his faithful companions, had seen him, conversed with him and shared food and drink with him after his death. They were the ones for whom it was appropriate to see him in this way; but it is fitting for all mankind, and was indeed for the sake of all, that he was thus manifested to them.

They encountered him alive from the dead in a manner which spoke to and transformed their faith, convincing them beyond all argument and against all odds that the power which had raised him from the dead had also glorified him beyond their immediate seeing. Their converts have no need to meet him in the way the disciples did, not because their faith is somehow outside history but because they are able to accept the original witness of those who had been decisively redirected by his visible, audible and tangible companionship in the Easter days: 'Through him you now have faith in God, who raised him from the dead and gave him glory for that very reason – so that you would have faith and hope in God'. The resurrection appearances were not an end in themselves: Jesus' coming to his own was the sign of his going to the Father rather than, like all men hitherto, remaining in death. Once the chosen had seen enough of him nobody else needs that kind of encounter, for in and through the original company the Spirit can be released for his work of drawing all mankind into true being as the body of Christ.

To disconnect faith from the original reports of God's action in Christ is to separate it equally from everything that has happened since. The raising of Jesus and his appearing to the disciples were the indispensable prelude to the coming of the Spirit; once the Spirit came the disciples entered on a new dimension of freedom in human living, an unprecedented and definitive intimacy with God. Ignore or belittle how on their own account they were brought to this radiation-point, and theology at once loses its grounding in the Spirit's witness, then and now. The Spirit brought to birth a new kind of consciousness, and this freeing of heart and mind was seen by the disciples as henceforth on offer to all who desired it enough to repent. The heart and substance of this new way of being was Jesus raised from the tomb.

If we say, as we must, that the change in the disciples after Golgotha is decisive for all that follows, we must take seriously their accounts of how that change came about. To say that John believed at the empty tomb and the rest when they saw the risen Lord does not *explain* their transformation but places it firmly in the setting of an identifiable relationship with him. This relationship has a specific, developing history from their first calling in Galilee to their Pentecostal preaching of him.

If we remove Jesus prematurely from recorded history by rejecting the resurrection narratives we maim this relationship, taking it out of history just at the point where the true shape of his life and death begins to be disclosed to them. They claimed that their empowering by the Spirit had to do with what they had seen to have happened to Jesus after Calvary. Their converts, and subsequent Christian generations, 'believed their report'. This report was of something at once uniquely extraordinary and uniquely comprehensive in the new meaning and dynamism it gave to all creation. The role of faith was therefore vital both in the origins of the report and in its spreading. The Easter events took Jesus' relationship with his disciples on to a new plane, while their reporting of those events to people who had not known Jesus sparked off and converged with the experiences and expectations of new believers. The new people thus came to share in that same relationship in the form in which it sustained the enspirited disciples after Whitsun.

When the matter is put in this way the role of faith both in the first disciples and in their converts may become clearer. For both, Jesus is with the Father in glory; for both he is Lord of creation. It is a spiritless version of this lordship which sees Jesus as a beneficent absentee landlord; faith in the New Testament's sense is a conviction of his abiding presence in the world. The raising of Jesus from the dead is from this point of view his becoming available in and for all those who are open to the reception of his Spirit. Because there is no adequate analogue for this form of presence we easily reduce it in our thinking to something merely ethereal, a kind of well-meaning wisp, a pale shadow of what he once had been when he walked the earth. Such a thin and impotent presence is clearly not at all what the New Testament is talking about. The disciples believed that Jesus was present in power wherever believers gathered, and that his lordship, established in his resurrection, was coming into its own wherever the word was preached, taught and celebrated: 'Where two or three are gathered together in my name, there am I in the midst of them.' He is regarded as more comprehensively and intimately present than ever before. A personal power formerly limited to acts of healing, exorcism and forgiveness in his immediate environment is now released everywhere his name is invoked; those who believe in him share him, share his life, in a way unimaginable in the Galilaean ministry. Anyone who turns to him, who says in the Spirit 'Jesus is Lord', is made free of this power as a member of his body.

Unless we can become attuned to this dimension of early Christian experience we shall reduce the New Testament's witness here to the merely metaphorical. In which case that witness would not be worth considering, for it would make of Jesus' presence after his ascension something less real than either his pre-crucifixion presence or his presence in the Easter days. That such is not the first believers' frame of reference is indicated by the fact that there is no hankering after those past forms of presence, so convinced are they of his continuous and active presence in the present. Moule points out that 'in John and Acts, the Spirit communicates and extends the presence of Christ . . . the experience of the Spirit by Christians does not . . . eclipse their experience of the presence of the living Christ himself. Quite the contrary.'[1] It is false to all the evidence to think that Jesus was more powerfully or really or precisely present when he was visible than thereafter. The opposite was in fact the case: the disciples had real faith in Jesus from their first calling, but no adequate appreciation of his significance in life and death until the Spirit was given. Only then was the truth of Jesus fully grasped and their relationship with him established in its most real and abiding form, as they found themselves able to appropriate his presence in becoming his body. Or it might be more accurate to say that his presence is of such a sort that he appropriates or incorporates them: 'I live now, not I, but Christ lives in me.' And it is the nature of this incorporation to spread itself.

There are eucharistic overtones to this theme which it would be beyond the scope of the book to pursue very far. But it is worth noting that the doctrine of the real presence of Christ in the eucharistic elements of bread and wine is bound in practice to have an idolatrous sense unless it is an aspect or extension of a living belief in the real presence of Christ in the body of believers and in all creation. Once this belief has atrophied it is in the nature of the case impossible to have a balanced attitude to the eucharistic elements, whether or not our theology is formally orthodox. In practice the elements come to be imagined as the exclusive housing of that presence of Christ no longer experienced in the multiform sharing which in principle believers have with one another, and with the wider church coming into being beyond the present boundaries of the eucharistic assembly.

The inexpressible mystery of the becoming of all things in Christ is consciously focussed in the action of the eucharist, the effective sign of that becoming. This sacrament is intended to confirm and expand the faith, hope and love already partially expressed in our common life and witness. I am not arguing against traditional teaching on the real presence, but attempting to situate that teaching in relation to the first Christians' overwhelming awareness of Christ in them, of themselves growing in Christ; an awareness which found expression in the exercise of a rich range of spiritual gifts used in complementarity with each other in love's work of building up the body. They sought in very diverse ways to promote a spreading realization of the risen Christ's urgent presence seeking to draw all to himself for their peace and his Father's glory.

'The priest brings Christ into the community', said a professor of theology anent what happens at Mass, with a degree of irritation at my extreme reluctance to take the point. The implications of such a view of the real presence, as indeed of priesthood, seem to me to be radically alien to the disciples' experience of the presence and power of the risen Lord. The taking and breaking and sharing of bread and wine is the supreme sign of Jesus' universal presence and power.

In the eucharist we are enabled by the Spirit to bring into consciousness the death of Jesus in its limitless power to save and raise up every element in this fallen world, that power which began to be recognized through his risen presence in its Easter form. We bring into the forefront of immediate consciousness his presence in all that is, epitomized in bread and wine, the vital nourishment of man the steward of creation. We have no need to bring him in from the outside, for in this sacrament he who is already our life and the true direction of the universe shares himself newly with us in a form which signifies his hidden presence everywhere and furthers our living out of his presence increasingly in every aspect of our lives. In this sense, if we so choose, we make him more present, for in love he is beholden to our response: 'Behold, I stand at the door and knock.' In the eucharist Jesus puts himself quite specifically at our disposal in the spirit of his death and resurrection, not merely in the elements but in the whole of our lives.

Thus we become the voice of creation praising God for his saving work of love in Jesus and pleading with the Lord Jesus to hasten his full and final coming for the consummation of all things. The eucharist, appropriately, can both humble and exalt us, cast us down in naked abjection and sweep us into the heart of the adorable mystery of God's love in Christ working through our world. It is the sacrament of the ineffable becoming of all things into that unimaginable unity which is most deeply and passionately desired by the heart of man at his most alive, which is in Christ. It is the sacrament of a man's death interpreted by his resurrection from the dead. Its dimensions so stretch our hearts and minds that we hardly know how to celebrate it, for we scarcely yet know how to live in Christ in our world, which is his. We need a real eucharist, and it often seems in the course of our fumbling attempts in that direction that such an event is far to seek.

In my experience the most real eucharist so far has been a requiem mass followed by a burial. This is hardly surprising, for life through death is what the eucharist is about. Immediately before his ordeal Jesus affirms that which is to be destroyed: his body. He affirms it in the sign of bread. His body is to flower in sacrament and community, and not in a merely idealistic way. He is not only to be with his own but in them, and they in him. Here the theme of the incorporation of the person who has died acquires an extended sense. Something material, bread, is to be the means of incorporation into Jesus. His living presence is to be embodied in this sign and shared with us so that we may become more and more the effective embodiment of his Spirit.

It is not easy to come to terms with a God who is immersed to this extent in the ambiguities of created life. It is much less taxing to think of the risen presence of Jesus as purely spiritual. Yet he clearly does not wish that his presence should be 'only an inner thought, something which one says to oneself'.[2] Much more than memory is at stake here: '. . . his presence is henceforth linked to a sign and to an object, to an action and to a thing . . .' The sacrament, the cross and the resurrection are the *same scandal*. Unfaith cannot cope with God's involvement with us at our roots: blood – bread – every last bit of us. So it is that we tend to hedge the eucharist, like death, with a kind of false reverence more akin to superstition. This distancing enables us to take ourselves less seriously than God takes us.

As in other aspects of Christian belief, a difficulty which at root has to do with self-acceptance is often mistakenly located in another sphere: 'The difficulty of the incarnation,' writes Sebastian Moore, 'is not in the dogmatic realm. It is the difficulty in a commanded self-acceptance that goes far beyond our limits of self-acceptance. It is the mystery of a God who comes upon us and loves us beyond the limits of our ego-organized potential.'[3] If this is true of the incarnation it is also true of the death and resurrection of Jesus, which enact the consequences of the incarnation; and supremely of the eucharist.

It is worth noting in this connection that in some mediaeval funeral liturgies the focus on the physical body 'has the effect both of giving life as we experience it a unique dignity and also of bringing the idea of eternal life very much into the present moment'.[4] Bread and wine in the eucharist are surely chosen to perform this double function of exalting our sense of present life and pointing us into the dimension of eternity. Close involvement with the dying and the death of someone you love may provide an initiation into the many-sided simplicity of this sacrament.

The death of Jesus has power to free us increasingly at every moment from the reign of sin and death: not from the fact of death but from the oppression of death as the final banality, the perennial joker in the pack, which in sin is all that death can be. The death of this one man is the release of all from that reign, as his friends quickly perceived, so strong and intimate are the links binding Jesus to all humanity. It remains for us to appropriate the Saviour, or to allow him to appropriate us, in order that his work, the remaking and drawing together of all things in love, may be finished.

Paul sees himself and those like him as 'always carrying in the body the death of Jesus, so that the life of Jesus may be manifested in our bodies. For while we live we are always being given up to death for Jesus' sake, so that the life of Jesus may be manifested in our mortal flesh.'

Thus in the working-out of the salvation achieved by the crucifixion, life and death are intimate and inseparable com-

panions, as Paul's experience clearly taught him. The renewed
and cleansed perception of the beloved which, as mentioned
earlier, is a central feature in the course of many bereavements,
can add a new dimension to the eucharist. Having to do with
the disentangling[5] both of the person who has died and of the
bereaved one from distortions and constrictions of spirit,
bereavement offers an immediate and powerful specification of
the continuing work of Jesus' death.

Equally, the potentially overwhelming effects of tragic loss
can be kept within appropriate bounds by truthful worship,
which does not short-circuit what has to be endured but offers
other and complementary perspectives intended to shape a
renewed heart and mind.

These reflections on the eucharistic aspect of resurrection-
faith point us back to the bed-rock fact that in the story of Jesus
and his disciples we are touching on things which, if they are to
be assimilated, must break our 'normal' categories of reality.
This story speaks of realities and possibilities strangely recognizable and yet otherwise uncharted.

Notes

1. Bearings

1. Colin Murray Parkes, *Bereavement*, Penguin Books 1978, is representative of this genre. Parkes acknowledges that some people are helped through bereavement by religious conviction, but expressly says that he is unable to give any account of this dimension. Elisabeth Kübler-Ross, *Death, the Final Stage of Growth*, Prentice-Hall 1984, was published too late for consideration here. The title indicates accurately a somewhat bolder approach from within the world of applied behavioural science than Parkes' contribution.

2. John Hick suggests this at the beginning of his book, *Death and Immortality*, Collins 1976.

3. Christopher Evans, *Resurrection and the New Testament*, SCM Press 1970, a well-mannered and moderate version of this tendency, could be considered representative. It should be added that within this type of writing there is a marked divergence among scholars as to which elements in the New Testament resurrection accounts are allowed more or less 'historicity'.

4. T.S. Eliot, *The Family Reunion*, Faber and Faber 1972.

5. It has surprised a number of interested enquirers to be told that when this exploration began I quite happily held what I would now describe as a misty modernistic interpretation of the resurrection stories in the Gospels. In the course of this work, I was shown that mist and mystery are hardly synonymous.

6. Such testimonies are quoted later in this book. Of those which have appeared subsequently, the autobiography of the Irish singer Mary O'Hara, *The Scent of the Roses*, Collins Fontana 1981, is especially vivid and poignant. To some extent the reader needs to read between the lines. Mary O'Hara often says 'more than she purposes', as do many other witnesses to death's gift.

7. This last phrase I owe to Dom Luke Suart, who said, 'You find in your own experience that you have become a person for ever.' Cf. the Johannine conviction that 'This *is* eternal life, to know you, the one true God, and Jesus Christ whom you have sent'.

8. This is not a declaration of final judgment. The way through hell to heaven is not foreclosed.

9. I would not want to confine this dynamic within the boundaries of the visible church, not least because this might exclude some of my witnesses!

10. Written and spoken records of such communication often breathe a stifling banality, which is characteristic of the workings of evil in many other contexts. On the other hand it can be equally destructive to rule out of court all desire for communion with the dead.

2. *The Wounded Self*

1. The *reductio ad absurdum* of this tendency is expressed with chilling and ludicrous impersonality and distancing in this extract from the Harrow Health District Handbook for 1978:

'The purpose of providing after-death services is to establish appropriate relationships that may possibly alleviate some of the risk of stress illness in relatives at a later stage. Relationships of this nature may also help to prevent loneliness which can be acute during the period immediately after death.

After a patient's demise the home nurse generally makes a few informal visits to the home in order to gradually terminate the relationships which are inevitably built up with the relative(s). Simultaneously the health visitor is introduced and gradually takes over and provides such support as may be necessary.

Avoidance of undue stress on relatives of bereaved

In the event of death the District Planning Team for Terminal Care decided that medical services, nursing services, social services and the Church should each be responsible for notifying the relevant persons involved within their own disciplines.

Services which are intermittently involved, such as chiropody and paramedical services, will be notified by the social work department.'

2. From a letter.

3. This phrase is akin to the even uglier 'grief work', which so emphasizes the task that it is in danger of losing sight of the gift.

4. Arthur W. Mielke, *Through the Valley*, Association Press, New York 1975, p. 89. It could be argued, though not perhaps pressed too far, that mourning is not really for the dead but for the 'survivors'. A widow said to me tearfully early in her bereavement: 'I'm not weeping for him, you know. I'm weeping for myself.'

5. Cf. The title of Peter Berger's book, *A Rumour of Angels*, Penguin Books 1971.

6. Mielke, *Through the Valley*. It could be argued that to invoke Paul here is to contradict my thesis of a sharp break in an already existing and close relationship. There is no evidence that Paul knew Jesus of Nazareth. An answer could be developed by suggesting that once Paul, 'a Pharisee of Pharisees', had heard of Jesus, he was caught up in a very intense relationship with him, that of the persecutor. This is the relationship context in which the risen Lord appeared to him.

7. J. Neville Ward, *Friday Afternoon*, Epworth Press 1976, p. 110.

3. *The Chosen*

1. Metropolitan Anthony Bloom, 'A Christmas Meditation', in *God and Man*, quoted in *The Tablet*, 23 December 1978.

2. I owe this insight to the Revd David Wynford Thomas.

3. Ulrich Wilckens, *Resurrection*, St Andrew Press 1977, p. 111.

This sentence concludes an extended pursuit of the search mentioned. Wolfhart Pannenberg, in *Jesus God and Man*, SCM Press 1968, dissents in the name of inter-testamentary apocalyptic. The next paragraph of my text suggests why I agree rather with Wilckens.

4. This phrase occurs at the opening of the second volume of Mervyn Peake's trilogy. This volume is entitled *Gormenghast*, Penguin Books 1970.

5. The notion of 'the shape of death' comes from Jaroslav Pelikan, *The Shape of Death*, Macmillan 1962.

6. Geoffrey Preston OP, *God's Way to be Man*, Darton, Longman and Todd 1978.

7. From the Easter Sequence *Victimae Paschali Laudes*, in the Latin Mass.

4. Permission to Flee

1. From W. R. Rogers, 'Resurrection: An Easter Sequence', published in *Europa and the Bull and other Poems*, Secker and Warburg 1952, p. 60.

2. Another evangelist places what seems the same episode much earlier in the story of Jesus. Its extreme verisimilitude at this point in the passion narrative convinces me of its rightful place here, whether or not a similar exchange had already occurred elsewhere, which is intrinsically probable.

3. I find myself wondering if this theme of sifting is an echo of Psalm 1. 4b:
> 'For they (the wicked) like winnowed chaff
> shall be driven away by the wind.'

5. Peter

1. Lord Hailsham, in a Radio 4 interview about his autobiography, *The Door Wherein I Went*, Collins 1975.

2. The germ of this idea came from an occasional piece by Bishop George Appleton in *The Daily Telegraph*.

6. The Beloved Disciple Remembers

1. O. Cullmann and F. J. Leenhardt, *Essays on the Lord's Supper*, Lutterworth Press 1959, p.42.

2. E.g. C. H. Dodd, *The Interpretation of the Fourth Gospel*, Cambridge University Press 1953, p. 394.

3. From a letter by the pseudonymous Richard quoted earlier.

4. Henri Nouwen, *In Memoriam*, Ave Maria Press, Notre Dame, Indiana 1980, p. 26.

5. Much more needs to be said here to move the debate about the tomb away from the sterile polarizaton which tends to characterize it, e.g. the continuing controversy around the views of the Bishop of Durham. Creative contributions have come from Sebastian Moore, in an article entitled 'An Empty Tomb Revisited', *Downside Review*, October 1981, pp. 239–47, and C. F. D. Moule, in his introduction to *The Significance of the Message of the Resurrection* for *Faith in Jesus Christ*, Studies in Biblical Theology, Second Series

8, SCM Press 1968, pp. 1–12. The point at issue is whether or not anything happens to and within the material universe in the raising of Jesus from the dead.

6. Some educationalists have seriously commended such study as likely to equip some school-children for the inner-city environment in which it is thought likely that they will spend the rest of their lives. It is at least implied that a more traditional literary curriculum would be irrelevant.

7. *Orphaning, Judgment and Glorification*

1. *The Grief Process*, SCM Press 1978, 'Epilogue: The death of Jesus and the grief of the disciples', pp. 343–8.
2. Geoffrey Preston, *God's Way to be Man*, p. 98.
3. P. J. Kavanagh, *The Perfect Stranger*, Quartet Books 1973, p. 180.
4. T. F. Torrance, *Space, Time and Resurrection*, Handsel Press 1976.
5. Cf. Thomas Merton's reflections on this story, in *Towards a Theology of Prayer, Cistercian Studies, Quarterly Review*, Volume XIII, 1978–3. His conclusion is that the theology of prayer begins when we understand that we are in trouble, and that we have a saviour with us whom we do not recognize.

8. *Seeing Again*

1. Jon Sobrino, *Christology at the Crossroads*, SCM Press 1978, p. 187, 'The resurrection does not eliminate the scandal. It elevates it to a mystery, making the questions as to why Jesus had to die and what God was doing on the cross more pointed.'
2. Cf. Christopher Neil-Smith, *The Exorcist and the Possessed*, James Pike 1974, p. 49.
3. Wilckens, *Resurrection*, pp. 13, 114, 121, is a case in point.
4. Stephen Verney, 'The Mystery of Resurrection', broadcast talk published in *The Listener*, 3 March 1977.
5. Julian of Norwich, *Revelations of Divine Love*, Methuen 1901, ch. 33.
6. Spiegel, *The Grief Process*, p. 348.
7. Sobrino, *Christology at the Crossroads*, p. 183.

9. *Joy*

1. Spiegel, *The Grief Process*, p. 348.
2. Kavanagh, *The Perfect Stranger*, p. 180.
3. W. B. Yeats, *Collected Poems*, Macmillan 1955, pp. 23–5.
4. Spiegel, *The Grief Process*, p. 348.
5. From the anthem *Salve Regina*, commonly translated as 'Hail, Holy Queen'.

10. *Neither Martyr nor Suicide*

1. G. J. O'Collins, *The Easter Jesus*, Darton, Longman and Todd 1973, pp. 126–30.

2. It is fascinating that in the posthumously published and fragmentary work by E. C. Hoskyns and N. Davey, *Crucifixion-Resurrection* (ed. Gordon S. Wakefield, SPCK 1981) is chosen as the title because Hoskyns judged that this hyphenated word best epitomized the heart of Christian faith. Although Hoskyns might well have been uncomfortable at some of my 'psychologizing', there are striking convergences between some of his material and mine.

3. Cf. Eberhard Jüngel, *Death, the Riddle and the Mystery*, St Andrew Press 1975, pp. 50–3, for a very sensitive analysis of the death of Socrates.

4. In the case of Jesus himself I should now want to modify this in the light of Sebastian Moore's view that Jesus, uniquely, had an unrepressed attitude to his own death, i.e. his death was *both* desired *and* dreaded. Cf. *The Inner Loneliness*, Darton, Longman and Todd 1982, pp. 97–9, for an account of how this affects the disciples.

5. Austin Farrer, *The Brink of Mystery*, SPCK 1976, p. 127.

6. Raymond Brown, *Jesus God and Man*, Geoffrey Chapman 1968, p. 66.

7. I would want to connect these words from the creed with the dead Jesus being in the heart of the earth, as in the sign of Jonah; and with the mediaeval theme of the harrowing of hell.

8. Sobrino, *Christology at the Crossroads*, p. 217.

9. Jüngel, *Death*, p. 78, makes the point that lapsing into a void of relationlessness, rather than merely being snuffed out, was central in the Jewish image of death.

11. The Poor, Sinners and the Sinless Man

1. Alan Watts, *Beyond Theology*, Vintage Books, New York 1964, passim.

2. Cf. Hoskyns and Davey, *Crucifixion-Resurrection*, ch. 8. Written long before liberation theology in any of its current senses was even dreamt of, Hoskyns' work provides an exciting and potentially salutary corrective to the sentimental or socio-economic moralism which pervades the contemporary debate.

3. It could even be argued that Judas was a mole in the John Le Carré sense, who had trouble in knowing which group he was really working for!

4. Martin Hengel, *Crucifixion*, SCM Press 1977.

5. Published as *Christianity and the World Order*, Oxford University Press 1979. Norman's abrasive approach tends to mask the good sense of some of his observations.

6. This bears on the multi-faith dialogue, and on the existence since the Second Vatican Council of a Roman Catholic Secretariat for Non-believers; but not in a way which confines the action of the Spirit to professing Christians.

12. Death-spasm

1. This presupposes an evolutionary view of creation, but does not entail any naively optimistic conclusion about the outcome in particulars. Much remains to be resolved in the continuing story of the crucified and risen Lord.

'God creates by redeeming', said my revered professor of Old Testament exegesis, Dominic Barthelémy OP.

2. Rogers, *Europa and the Bull*, p. 68.

3. Rogers, *Europa and the Bull*, p. 66. It is interesting that Rogers began as a Presbyterian minister, although his somewhat turbulent life took him out of the ministry and into the BBC, whose sound radio introduced me to his poems.

4. Pierre Teilhard de Chardin writes in *The Future of Man*, Collins 1964, p. 23: 'Little by little the idea is coming to light in Christian consciousness that the "phylogenesis" of the whole man, and *not merely the "ontogenesis" of his moral virtues*, is hallowed, in the sense that the charity of the believer may more resemble *an impulse of constructive energy* . . .'(my italics).

5. Elizabeth signed the death warrant of Mary Queen of Scots, but did not directly authorize its despatch to Fotheringay.

6. Ben F. Meyer, *The Aims of Jesus*, SCM Press 1979.

7. A typical example is the presentation of Jesus as 'the man for others', which by-passes his character as the obedient one, the one who enters into his own 'ultimate poverty' (Hoskyns, op. cit., ch. 8).

8. Pannenberg, *Jesus: God and Man*, p. 97.

9. Dr David Ford helped me to see that it was appropriate for Peter to be pressed to declare his love, and to declare it in this threefold way in inverse symphony with his threefold denial, if he was to be launched on his vocation.

13. The Hinge of Memory

1. Oliver Lyttelton, *From Peace to War*, quoted in Paul Fussell, *The Great War and Modern Memory*, Oxford University Press, p. 327.

2. Rudolf Otto, *The Idea of the Holy*, Oxford University Press 1931. Dominic Barthelémy taught us in Fribourg long ago that *fear of the Lord* is the central moral quality in the Old Testament. It centres everything on the living God, thus reining in even the highest moral wisdom, which would otherwise collude with an idolatrous human self-sufficiency. Yet this theme barely features in expositions of Christian ethics, perhaps because it is confused with that very different and craven fear which is cast out by perfect love.

3. Arthur Janov, *The Primal Scream*, Sphere Books 1973, passim. The later work of Dr Frank Lake in the area of recovering pre-natal experience points in a similar direction.

4. Joseph Conrad, *Lord Jim*, Penguin Books 1971.

5. The argument here stresses the effects of this condition on the blinkered disciple. A more complete picture would spell out the fact that in so far as there is an element of self-destruction in a static discipleship there is necessarily some other-destruction as well, whatever the conscious intention. In my way of being I became an intransigent contradiction of the unity I sought. There are no short cuts to freedom, still less any neutrality, and the social effects of such a disjunction as I have described are painfully apparent.

6. Rowan Williams, 'Resurrection', Darton, Longman and Todd 1982, pp. 41–3, says that the risen Jesus *gave the disciples back their past*. This epitomizes something crucial to my whole approach, so much so

that I thought for a moment that Williams had made my book expendable.

7. Lily Pincus, *Death and the Family*, Faber and Faber 1976, pp. 124–7.

14. The Future of Memory

1. Rogers, *Europa and the Bull*, p. 62.

2. This is not to dismiss Marx or Freud from serious consideration. Elements of both are in any case part of the air we all breathe, even if we imagine ourselves 'innocent' of their pervasive influence.

3. Edmund Blunden, *Undertones of War*, quoted in Fussell, *The Great War*, pp. 259–60.

4. E.g. Fussell, *The Great War*, passim. This view is made more pointed by the floating in theological circles of the rhetorical question 'Is theology possible after Auschwitz?'. Implicit here is a denial of the power of Jesus' death: certain horrors are seen as so overwhelming as to rule out any hopeful conclusion.

15. Dead Ends

1. In a letter to Mervyn Peake about Peake's *Gormenghast*, published in Maeve Gilmore and Shelagh Johnson, *Mervyn Peake: Writings and Drawings*, Academy Editions 1974, p. 83.

2. Hubert Richards, *The First Easter: What Really Happened?*, Collins/Fount 1976.

3. For the sake of balance it should be noted that Richards is peculiarly unguarded here. More cautious interpreters sympathetic to his starting-point go to greater lengths to avoid any suggestion of conscious falsification on the part of the evangelists. They would still come under the strictures of my next paragraph.

4. Hans Küng, *On Being a Christian*, Collins 1977, p. 233.

5. This sentence is the heart of my argument, with the conclusion that this mutation is on offer to us as the effective sign of the destiny of humanity.

6. James D. G. Dunn, *Jesus and the Spirit*, SCM Press 1975, p. 96.

7. Ibid., p. 131.

8. The use of this phrase in such an inappropriate context betrays the inveterate human tendency to reduce mystery to moralism. The truth of the matter is that the disciples begin from Pentecost onwards to manifest a deep *desire* to share what has happened with all who can hear their word. True love is of its nature contagious.

16. What Difference Does It Make?

1. From a poem by Dom Luke Suart published in the Downside School magazine *The Raven*, Eyre and Spottiswoode, Autumn 1964.

2. Rosemary Haughton is eloquent on this in *The Passionate God*, Darton, Longman and Todd 1981, passim.

3. There is a tendency to reduce this hymn to behavioural precepts; it is rather a *description* of the fruits of true love, of how love behaves.

4. C. F. D. Moule, *The Origin of Christology*, Cambridge University Press 1977, p. 103.

5. Cf. Sebastian Moore, *The Fire and the Rose are One*, Darton, Longman and Todd 1980, pp. 151–8. Moore exposes and moves beyond a common confusion about the significance of the titles given to Jesus in the New Testament.

6. Mielke, *Through the Valley*, pp. 71–2.

7. For a clear positive exposition of this doctrine in the context of the historical difficulties Protestants have had with it, cf. P. Y. Emery, *The Communion of Saints*, Faith Press 1966. Emery writes as a convinced Protestant.

8. C. S. Lewis, *The Screwtape Letters*, Bles 1942, Ch. 15.

17. Predisposition and Revelation

1. Bernard Lonergan, *Insight*, Darton, Longman and Todd 1958.

2. Pierre Teilhard de Chardin, *The Phenomenon of Man*, Collins 1960.

3. Peter Medawar among scientists, and Laurence Bright OP among theologians, are names that spring to mind.

4. Pierre Teilhard de Chardin, *The Future of Man*, Collins 1964, p. 22.

5. Harry Williams, *True Resurrection*, Mitchell Beazley 1972.

18. Real Presence

1. Moule, *The Origin of Christology*, pp. 114–15.

2. F. J. Leenhardt, in Cullmann and Leenhardt, *Essays on the Lord's Supper*, p. 43.

3. Sebastian Moore, *The Crucified is No Stranger*, Darton, Longman and Todd 1977, pp. 5–6.

4. Graeme Griffin, *Death and the Church: Problems and Possibilities*, Dove Communications, Melbourne, Australia 1978.

5. Cf. Rosemary Haughton, *The Drama of Salvation*, SPCK 1976, p. 131. The word 'disentangling' occurs in the final chapter, where Rosemary Haughton powerfully pursues the question of why the dénouement of the drama of salvation has to be a death.